MICHAEL
BRADBURN-RUSTER

# THE SHADOW OF GABRIEL'S WING

POEMS

FOREWORD

BY

ALAIN SAINT-SAËNS

2021

Published in the USA by The University Press of the South. Printed in France by Monbeaulivre.fr.

E-mails:unprsouth@aol.com;universitypresssouth@gmail.com

Visit our award-winning web pages:

www.unprsouth.com

www.punouveaumonde.com

Michael Bradburn-Ruster.

The Shadow of Gabriel's Wing.

First Edition in English. Poetry Studies, 57.

Foreword by Alain Saint-Saëns.

Cover Art by Ana María Calatayud. ('Man and Woman Contemplating the Moon.' Painting by Caspar David Friedrich. ca. 1824. Reproduced with Permission).

180 pages.

1. Literature. 2. Poetry. 3. United States. 4. Romantic Poetry. 5. Mysteries of Soul. 6. Mystical Contemplation. 7. Ancient History. 8. Greek Mythology. 9. Alain Saint-Saëns. 10. Michael Bradburn-Ruster.

ISBN: 978-1-952799-09-9 (European Edition: 2021)

# FOREWORD

*The Shadow of Gabriel's Wing,* Michael Bradburn-Ruster's collection of poetry, makes me think of French painter Jean-Antoine Watteau's painting, 'Embarkation for Cythera.' It is an invitation to travel through history and mythology, dreams and fantasy, soul and love. The Notes at the end of the volume reveal the acuity of the research that the poet completed while composing his pieces of creative work. There, Michael reveals that he is all at once an historian and a theologian, a phenomenologist and an archaeologist.

But above all, he is a magnificent poet. Rhythm and musicality, silences and echoes, guide us through the labyrinth of his artisanal, luminous verses, as Ariadne's thread guided Theseus on his way back, after having killed the Minotaur. 'Darkness sings,' writes the poet. Maybe so ; nevertheless, the moon enlightens shadowy territories, as it does in Caspar David Friedrich's painting, 'Man and Woman Contemplating the Moon' (1824), with which the poet chose to adorn his book's front cover. References to German Romanticism are evident throughout the book, in currents of wit, humour, and the adulation of beauty. Bradburn-Ruster's poetry furthermore reminds me of Friedrich Hölderlin's, so much influenced by Ancient Greek poets Alcaeus and Asclepiades of Samos, and Novalis', another German Romantic poet he quotes to qualify his own poetry: 'The communion between the finite and the infinite.'

By many aspects, Michael Bradburn-Ruster, a mature man and poet, is 'The Wanderer above the Sea of Fog' (1817), as depicted in another of Caspar David Friedrich's paintings. In our terrible days of Covid-19 pandemic, Michael Bradburn-Ruster examplifies 'The Function of the Poet', as defined by French poet Victor Hugo in 1830: 'In such times gone awry, from far / The poet brings tidings of better days.'[1]

*ALAIN SAINT-SAËNS*
Poet and Literary Critic,
Corresponding Member,
Academy of Letters, Bahia, Brazil

---

[1] *Le poète en des jours impies /*
*Vient préparer des jours meilleurs.*

# THE SHADOW OF GABRIEL'S WING

## POEMS

According to the twelfth-century Sufi Suhrawardī, the angel Gabriel possesses a right wing of pure Light, while the left is mottled with dark: this imperfect world below is the "song and shadow of Gabriel's wing."
—Sachiko Murata

...Or was this an angel showing me
A world that none of us can see?
—Anna Akhmatova

I. ***Mirabilium*** 1
Aperture 3
*Sospiri* 4
Ananta Raga 5
The Omnivoyant Gaze 10
Legible 11
*Masala Chai*: Alchemical Geography 12
Perpetual Oblation 14
Angel of the Spandrel 15
*Sfumato: Ars Pingendi* 16
Monastery 17
Because They Have Forsaken 18
Meditation on an Artichoke 19
Gull-Feather Fallen 21
A Recipe for Sangría 22
*De natura sonoris* 23
Communion 24
*Lux Mundi* 25
Cartography 26
A Gift 27
*Winterreise* 28
A Daughter at the Shore 29
Matin Bonfire 30
Patience 31
Elixir 32
Intrepid Souls 33

II. ***Legendarium*** 35
A Ring of Ancient Stones 37
Unholy Territory 38
Traces of a Mother's Mythology 40
Xenophanes 41
Letter from Tarsus 43
Encounter with Asterion 45
Tomb of a Carthaginian Priestess 47
Phidias in Olympia 48
Leopardi 52
Scorpion 54
Darkling (*Eleodes Obscurus*) 55

The Count 59
A Notebook of 1920 60
Seventy Years 62
True Tongue 64
A Lemon 65
Invisible Glance 67
With No Abode 68
Tabor 69
The Vacant Cross 70
Easter Vigil 71
Carved Virgin 72

III. ***Eros/Algos*** 73
Apotheosis of Earthly Love 75
Surrender 76
A Moment Fastened 77
Aubade 78
Concourse 79
Waiting 81
Nuptials 82
Ecstasy 83
Winter Consolation 85
What Remained 85
Cleft and Clasp: A Retort 86
Ode to The Letter *V* 87
Remnants 90
Cunnilingus 91
Presages 92
An Old Greek Nun Recalls Her Youth 94
Before the Summer 95
Renovation 96
*Tenebrae* 97
Incarnation: A Gloss 98
Nocturnal Flight 100
Again… 100
Palimpsest 101
Ruthless Ardor 103

IV. ***Lachrymae Rerum*** 105
Undisclosed: A Plea for Melancholy 107
Hidden Bounty 108
A Daughter's Kite 109
Familiar Faces 110
November Heaven 111
Crepuscular Flock 112
A Mother Mourns a Miracle 113
Counsel From An Apparition 114
Unperishing 115
Insatiable 116
Vespers at Mendocino 117
Autumn Nocturne 119
Exile 121
A Garden Regained 122
Forever, Ephemeral 124
A Teardrop 125
Winter Affinity 126
Old Ones 127
The Widow Alone 128
A Soldier Writes Home 129
Lachrimæ Pavan 130
*Nafs* 130
Lesson in Mourning 131
Expectant Autumn 132
Requiem For A Scholar 133
In Retrospect: Divorce 134
Remorse 135
An Elder Nears the End 136
*Fanā'* 136
An Oasis 137

V. ***Canticum Mysterium*** 139
153 - Notes to Poems
167 – *Acknowledgements*

# Mirabilium

*Meantime let wonder seem familiar...*
—Shakespeare

## Aperture

*for Geneviève Laurenceau*

The water in the ancient well
is cold, and whether it is clean
or not, the clouds alight and sip

the dark. Their swanlight shapes align
with roots the mirror veils, a wisp
or lobe aloft in visual

accord with filaments that seep
through fracture, gnarled fibers, sullen
meanders dense with thirst. Jewel

of realms that coalesce, tranquil
sonata, icon's echo, clasp
us in your faithful discipline.

## Sospiri

*(Elgar)*

*for Justine Kennedy*

*Everything is a sigh...*
—Nicola Benedetti
*...the poetry...of longing.*
—August Wilhelm Schlegel

On the vast breath of time the forests rise
and ocean surges—forms congeal, dissolve.
A bloom on stem, a comely limb: brief fires
that flare and fade on tides of toil and love.
Might the whispered caress of virgin snow
or the leopard's perilous grace endure?
We—wonder's witnesses—linger but now,
cherish what perishes, yearn... surrender,
while galaxies unfathomed scintillate
in realms that never will remember us.
How else respond? Just lift the hand in flight
to graze that swell our breast cannot embrace,
offer a gasp of awe, a poignant sigh:
invocation of all we cannot say.

## Ananta Raga

*for Ravi and Anoushka Shankar*

*The entire world gleams...*
– Abhinavagupta

Out of divinity's
silence, rags of echoes,
vines that trace vestiges
of verse on barren stone:
within the desert cave
flows a womb of water,
amid a nest of coals
flowers a tongue of flame,
and music without end
seems again to begin.

Not merely aesthetic:
sublimely ascetic:
listening, we forget
to remember our grief,
and bondage of pleasure
yields to beauty's nectar,
no longer erotic:
ecstatic sacrifice.

*Alāp*: veil raised in sleep,
glimpse of the sacred voice,
five fingers transfigured
into a lotus throne,
each finger become one
of the five syllables

carving the path that leads
beyond light and darkness.

Saffron and turquoise join
sapphire and turmeric:
so fire affirms poise,
soft rain murmurs passion,
*purusha* and *prakriti*
embrace, intertwine,
unleash earth's hidden streams,
give birth to tender grain,
awaken the flame inscribed
in the heart's ashes:
pulverized sun, mirror
of moon's liquefaction,
palace of symbols
whose ruins invent gardens.

*Tāla* and *rāgā*:
from the rhythm arises
the aroma. *Rasavant*,
flavour of rapture,
fragrance that transmutes time
into eternity,
as four hands scintillate,
dance in Chidambaram:
Golden Hall, cloudless heart,
still center of the world.

With one thousand eight hundred
names you praise the One,
Vīrabhadra dancing
over the blazing ghats
on whose burning-ground

corpses nurture the cosmos:
visions and illusions
created, cremated.
When the cup was shattered,
water filled the parched mouth.
Body smeared with ashes:
shadow that perishes;
concealed in that body
presence without measure.

Young woman, ancient man
drink from the same river
whose undivided source
reflects a single face:
Ardhanārīshvara,
radiant amalgam
both female and male, form
of the unmanifest
Lord who bestows fever
and banishes evil.

Kālidasa knew: one
of His eight modes is sound.

*Tablā* and *sitār*:
weft and warp of earth's carpet.
Drum that consecrates time,
dissolves it in color,
clay filled with flakes of breath,
articulate petals.
Gourd that becomes *garbha*
trembling with seeds of stars:

instrument of knowledge,
devotional compass,

incandescent tissue
of sympathetic strings,
utterance of incense,
delicate plenitude.

The daughter does not dwell
in her father's shadow:
both are inhabited
by the pulse of planets
and the lakes' quiescence,
by night's luminous tide,
serenities of snow,
sonority of smoke,
sorrow's fathomless web,
clarity's vertigo.
Body: vibrant crystal,
tree where our lives alight.
On the branch the ripe fruit
became bird, and took flight;
now she, like her father,
resides in resonance.

Once the man vanishes
melody will not cease
to kindle the silence,
sustain and ravish us,
return us to that place
we never discovered,
where grace alone abides,
horizon and heaven.

*Anugraha* is all:
with East and West erased,
farewell turns to summons:
*Come, embody the art*

*of Natarāja,*
*divulge Pythagoras' dream:*
*reveal the mystery*
*ever invisible.*
*Not matter – music weaves*
*the substance of the world.*

## The Omnivoyant Gaze

*...a certain secret*
*and hidden silence*
*beyond all faces...*
—Nicholas of Cusa

What colour were those eyes in the icon
Nicholas of Cusa sent to the monks?
Vanished: returned beyond time, to abide
as Gaze bereft of pigment, in that depth
whose Countenance is sought on every path.
Form that enfolds all forms, vision inscribed
in the vibrant ashes of the phoenix,
in purblind flesh when the bread is broken.

## Legible

*... creatures are shadows,*
*echoes and pictures...*
—St. Bonaventure
*... like a reflection in clear water*
*or in a stainless mirror.*
—Adi Śankara

The swallow's signature dissolves,
a flourish cast upon the dusk—
as mind through time plunges, soars, veers.
Centuries: visions, heaps of char.
Śankara and Bonaventure,
revelations and reveries.
Worlds: images wrought of music
in the wake eternity cleaves.

## Masala Chai: Alchemical Geograph

They nestle in your palm like insects culled
inert from dusty sills, inklings the mind
might winnow from caprices half recalled,
or dainty shards the potter seeks to mend.

Analogies at best banal: you cup
instead the latent fragrance of the world.
Cast the spices in water… let landscape
simmer forth – scroll of cinnamon, prelude

to sultry forests – the spiked buds of clove
an aromatic archipelago –
cardamom capsules whose dark seeds resolve
into vertigos of verdure. In league

with loam and bird and mist they weave a map
invisible, in harmonies of smell
that summon realms at once torrid and damp:
Molucca, Malabar, Guatemala…

The hands of Muslims, Hindus, Sikhs, Christians,
have conspired to proffer this gift. Pour in
the milk that once was pasture, then finesse
the sugar nourished by Veracruz rain.

And once the fluid ivory shimmers
like Muga silk, strew tea leaves from Assam
to form a cryptic poem that marries
Kamarupi script and wise axiom,

soon lost in the abode of clouds you stir.
Quench the fire. Wait, till territories blend.
Then savor the light from our single star
refracted through Earth's myriad garland.

## **Perpetual Oblation**

*(in terram visionis)*

*...for now I know...*
—Gen. 22:12

Once more that voice, "Where is the lamb?"
As age ordains, your sinews waned,
the Land of Vision beckoned: Rise—
for prior gifts were not enough.
Bear now again the fire, the knife;
the third day you will lift your eyes.
*Shall yet the ram await its wound?*
And still you answer, "Here I am."

## Angel of the Spandrel

*(Kölner Dom)*

Relinquish time. Forget all dates –
the lapse of centuries erased.
Your gaze ascending to the poise
that dwells between arcade and vault,
behold: a creature spun from light,
whose echo here is flame. Expose
the mirror shrouded in your breast
amid that murk of craven doubts.

## *Sfumato:* *Ars Pingendi*

*...intellegitur plus semper quam pingitur...*
—Pliny, *Nat. Hist.*, XXXV.36.74

Caressing curve of cheek, contour of neck:
gradations, diminutions—smoke or scent?
A nuance not achieved by mere technique,
though pigment has been culled from flakes of night.
To render what appears will not suffice,
for shadows must disclose that unseen form:
the fragile fate that haunts the vital face,
that hour beyond the limits of this frame.

Allow the ambiguities to bloom,
let pure penumbra orient your brush.
Evoke, between the absence and the gleam,
exquisite flesh upon the verge of ash:
the presence of a plenitude unguessed,
inhabited by our prophetic ghost.

## Monastery

(*San Antolín de Bedón, Asturias*)

*for José Luis Puerto*

I.

Imagine tides through centuries:
collapse of crest, caress of surf
not fallen on some idle ear
but interleaving with the swell
of chant that lingers for awhile
and vanishes in mists of prayer.
Two shaggy horses graze the reef
of meadow; shipwrecked souls arise.

II.

Declining light, world fallen still.
It's he who leads, as one immune
to haunting whispers, yet alive
to glint and echo of the lost
we seek in flooded pasture, blast
of wind these oaks and ruins cleave.
What words are his and which were mine?
As all is gift, we may not tell.

## Because They Have Forsaken

*Jer. 17:13;*
*John 8:1-11*

Deception played no part in my design,
unwelcome weed among intended herbs.
Desire?—oh, yes... his limbs like freshly risen
bread, those curls fragrant as a wreath of bays.

That other one, to whom wedlock confined
me, spurned all tenderness or grace, fulfilled
his pleasure with the grimace of a fiend.
Yet it was I who faced them now: defiled,

encompassed by a coil of eager stones.
Though one who sat apart leaned forward, tracing
figures at his feet, then rose. A brightness
infused his face, his simple words a song

that married mercy with reproach, familiar
yet somehow strange. He bent to write again.
Not one blow fell: their triumph lay in failure.
He turned to bless us all, but they were gone;

our gazes joined, our murmurs interlaced...
Whatever he'd inscribed upon the dust
that veiled the temple floor had been erased.

## Meditation on an Artichoke

*In mem. REB*

Beyond the blooming steam a fist of scales
appears: you might anticipate a duel,
assume the imbricated shields enclose
a tiny yet ferocious citadel

where any breach is met with eager blade.
But do not take the surface, thorn, or blemish
for proof of rancor – you will be beguiled
by mere illusion. Penetrate the mesh

with elegance: your task is not to conquer,
but leaf by leaf begin your pilgrimage,
as if a song had conjured some obscure
desire to leave the forest's fearsome edge

and seek the fabled center. Fingers detach
the pages of a calendar; each bract
of leather turns to petal at your touch,
conforms to tongue's design, the intricate

fecundity of time transfigured here,
as teeth peel earthy pulp with ginger skill
to find the savors of the spring perdure
when outmost autumn flesh yields to paschal

inwardness: this globe you deemed a rigid
phalanx clad in stolid olive fiber
guards a precious quarry of supple jade
like finespun satin in your mouth. Lay bare

at last the hooded mystery that seals
the final secret, hasten to inherit
– beneath anemone's enfolded bristles –
what you from habit choose to call the heart,

and let not lips alone but soul caress
that velvet throne, the once-pavilioned place
which mirrors what no pleasures offer us:
that cherished womb where life began to pulse.

## Gull-Feather Fallen

I never saw the bird, nor heard its flight,
assuming it was ever there at all;
perhaps the drowsy breeze began to wilt
and snatched up in one final flare of style
the weightless blade that spun down, helical
and delicate, to grace my path. I knelt
to a flame the color of fog, a quill
whose filament was pearl, articulate
of cloud, and seas' immensity, of mist
and grassy headland stooping to the shore:
that feather filled my hand until a mast
loomed out of loneliness, and with a sheer
bloom of canvas, my heart—long pent and blind—
unfurled and glimpsed the day's uncharted land.

## A Recipe for Sangría

*for Bill Rubin*

A single orange, a tender peach, sliced
and cubed, respectively, then strewn with care
into the pool of grenadine, at least
until the fibers of the flesh flicker

with crimson. Do not resort to sugar
or be tempted by ignoble wine, if
shame is of concern; most adepts figure
syrup, fruit and grape give ripeness enough.

And to bring the elixir to piquant
perfection necessitates liquid jade
nestled in limes' crescent flames: opaque knit
of succulence, tartness artfully wedged.

That waiter in Salamanca might tell
you there is one essential—you must lace
it with gin—though further west a hostile
wince would deem this innovation reckless

heresy. Yet fine mineral water
is needful, and whatever ritual
you observe, the glimmers of a guitar
should invade your hands. Let this nectar chill

until the colour turns melancholy
and night comes drifting like a sable swan.
Taste, then, those woeful joys that fill your skull
as the sun's blood and earth's ghost intertwine.

## *De natura sonoris*

*for Jorge Martínez García*

Like some forsaken, trodden bloom, the ear
hourly suffers bitter cacophonies
and brutal assaults – discords that smother
our souls. Rasp and shriek, or skirl that profanes

the innocent air: lithic clatter of
trucks, drill's clangor, asthmatic ecstasy
of pump and vacuum conspire to bereave
us of that kindly silence that kissed us

awake. Yet listen: the interstices
of that strident web hum; harmonies
abound. Ocean's lapping sleep entices
peace, rhythmic raven wings conjure romance,
a lone flute lofts a song fragrant as cloves,
the majestic planet mutely revolves.

## Communion

*for Adrian Pearce*

This I could not understand
even then – after mountains
and rivers had long denied
me the ancient litanies
known by rain perhaps or wind
alone: not anonymous
laws to which we dumbly nod
assent, but luminous names
once called forth this adamant
world into song, that odd paths
might converge on the same note
and unravel into depths
where slopes met and streams gathered
in praise of the seamless thread.

## *Lux Mundi*

You seep through dawn's hidden chambers of air
and awake the wind to phantom rovings,
stir finch to flight, lure reptile from his lair
to quaff the color, savor, scent of things.
All measures deepen at your touch, emerge
from night's immensity and flux toward form,
perfume, vermilion, music; the warm verge
of heaven falls even to root and worm.
Even through dark you delve: the inner mire –
fraught and fruitless with gloom – you transmute, as
green to gold the apple's alchemic fire,
or as ever you gleam in my love's eyes.
O, beneath our skin Socrates' prayer spin:
Ripen all souls to loveliness within.

## Cartography

*for Paul Scofield*

Your voice awakens worlds: each word a road
beckoning toward some perplexing junction,
while fleeting gestures conjure a brief mode
of divinity's daunting reflection.
Questions harbour silent currents roaming
(*what shore awaits us?*) toward secret limits
where answers lurk engraved in the foaming
tide of a sea agleam with amulets.

We glimpse how soul's true nature is revealed
in the shape of a mouth, unfathomed realm
where kiss or curse hovers, obscurely veiled,
while lyrical winds tremble at its brim:
for body is pressed of diverse musics,
though it inhabit a region of masks.

## A Gift

*for Myrna*

She returned from her solitary walk
with solar embers still in her eyes, and
spindrift kisses that whispered me awake
so I might touch what she'd found in the sand:

a small, flat stone dropped into my palm, round
as an old doubloon or enchanted disk,
with hues that evoked avocado rind.
What did it mean to her? I dared not ask,

but reckoned it, instead, as rich a troth
as any ring or precious gem could be,
for she had sensed some deeper, wondrous worth
and plucked it from the wild surf of the bay.

It must have seemed a planet within reach,
astray among countless damp gold stars; fate
deciding she alone should stroll the beach
and find the sky wide open at her feet.

## *Winterreise*

*for Balthazar*

We journey all day through ivory regions,
pine boughs clotted with cold foam; stark, subtle
arabesques of aspen lace; ice conjoins
lake with emerald, lightning with crystal.

Toward evening the light turned wistful, austere;
then the night sky's phantasmal cliffs crumbled,
clouds belched frantic shreds of alabaster
and the road smothered in the moon's wild blood.

The car edged along the highway, while I
clung to the wheel, too tense almost to hear
my son's words—"Though it's cold, snow's a holy
gift for children... an angel like dark air

told me in a dream." No time to destroy
illusions: the way before us, diffuse
and veiled, led into depths of mystery,
where soft wings fluttered toward my weary face.

## A Daughter at the Shore

*(Bixby Beach)*

*for Elizabeth*

Across the creek, bare-soled, the soaring bridge
behind. I've brought no food: we're all we need.
No fog tonight, to sift the surf's harangue
as sun declines unseen beyond a quilt
of cloud. She prances, flings her arms, delight
becomes a song, her face an offering.
She murmurs, "When you die, I will pretend
you're still alive." We watch the dusk emerge.

## Matin Bonfire

*for Sasha*

A phantom moon: the early sky
saturates our worlds with sapphire,
while kindling sprouts a dozen wisps
that singe the garden's frosty air,
scintillae celebrate the year
to come. Then, flames: seraphic spies
to witness our will to suffer
the wonder we may not forsake.

## Patience

*for Sasha*

To pause, point out small marvels to a child:
the foam where surf seeps into thirsty sand,
that enigmatic chart engraved on bark,
those primal patterns at the geode's core.
And if she drifts away – seems not to care –
remember how all seeds, before they break
into shimmering field or grove, descend
to seeming sleep, that beauty be fulfilled.

## Elixir

*for Elizabeth Ursula*

*Abide yet, though your voyage calls away...*
—Homer, *Odyssey* (I.471)

Eternity, though not within our grasp,
Lies undisclosed with every breath we share,
Instilling fire into our feeble sap,
Zealous hope into souls always unsure,
Adrift upon ships of luminous dust.
Beauty pronounces the ultimate shore,
Elaborates the sacred journey sought:
Through fathomless calm or infernal storm,
Hear the aspen whisper? and stars recite?

Unknown to us, a realm beyond all dream
Replies to riddles we may never ask,
Shapes water's flow and flight of bird, to frame
Ubiquitous grace, haunting every risk:
Lavish elixir urging us to sip
Ageless presence that time cannot forsake.

## Intrepid Souls

*Don't be afraid,* the mother cries,
her voice of mist leaping from shore
to span the crystal of the lake
where skaters dance: *The ice will hold...*
*Be not afraid,* the angel hailed
a girl whose breasts would bear the milk
of deathless love: a cynosure
undaunted by the winter freeze.

# Legendarium

*...Le pays qui ne sait que l'éternel...*
—Yves Bonnefoy

## A Ring of Ancient Stones

(*Pentre Ifan, Pembrokeshire*)

What haunts here bears us no malice:
not dire tomb, but time's gaunt synod.
Cathedral of the nebulae,
astronomy and ritual.
Our coats cannot defeat the chill
that whispers some lost syllable.
Do such mists arise or descend,
where thoughts descry the fathomless?

## Unholy Territory

*Et in Arcadia ego...*

"Ask any of the locals. They can tell
you how sometimes a man plowing his field
unearths a monstrous bone from that battle,
when the Olympian gods nearly failed.

They could take you to where the ground smolders
still from the molten metal of Hephaestus,
and Hecate's torch. No visitor dares
question the tale: to do so manifests

a wanton disregard for sacred truths.
Heed this, whatever the length of your stay:
do not suggest the vapors of Bathos
result from volcanic activity;

never venture to claim those bones belong
to mammoths, citing the region's museum
in your defense. We would see that you cling
to notions that are not welcome, presume

to a vision of things no foreigner
is entitled to hold. Those who molest
us with doubts aim only to ruin our
paradise, which the gods' triumph once blessed.

And should you hint that the conflict took place

on Italian soil, as Euripides
did, consider yourself fragile as glass:
for there cannot be two Arcadias,

nor more than one version of history.
Yes, those serpent-footed giants from Thrace
were vanquished here: no need to go astray
unless, friend, you intend to pay the price."

## Traces of a Mother's Mythology

She never offered legends: those Argive
ships and brutal heroes, the Golden Fleece
or Sword in Stone. Instead, she uttered names
unknown: a litany of cherished friends
whose ordinary faults and fates were grounds
for grace. Remembrance fails me, effort numbs
intent—mere remnants consecrate their loss.
Beyond the grave, she continues to give.

## Xenophanes

(c. 570-c.475 BC)

Beyond conjecture (fragments, fancies, hints)
we know but little of his ninety years.
Wandering poet, mystic, satirist:
born, like all mortals, of earth and water.

His noble, native Colophon is strewn
among three hills, its feared cavalry fled:
bereft those twelve towers of the ruin,
that temple of Demēter's rites, crumbled.

No trace abides of might or Mysteries.
Like fragrant ointment, wine, and frankincense…
Gone. Yet shells and fossils of sea creatures
he found so far from shore outlast the stones'

once proud geometries – as his bold verse,
whose volume centuries reduced to shards
that brute vicissitudes could not erase –
survives Olympus' realm of phantom gods.

His purpose did not stoop to emulate
the mirthful shape of Polymnastus' voice,
nor that graced murmur of Mimnermus' flute,
but harbored a more intricate device:

the art to pierce the veil, dispel the vain
idolatry of figments we impose
upon the formless face of the Divine –

as wisdom might deplore (though not despise)

the cult of games: footrace and chariot
wrestling and pentathlon – specious glories
unfit for thought. Far less should we narrate
the follies, thefts, deceits our common lore

ascribes to godliness. *We must amend*
*the mind: relinquish Homer's fabulous*
*conceits, yarns of epic spite and honeyed*
*passions – aspiring to a sphere of bliss*

*more finely spun, lest we devote our breath*
*to vagaries, and labor to confine*
*amid the vapors of our wits a truth*
*beyond the brim of time, a span we feign*

*to fathom in the mirror of our whims.*
*For semblance merely stains the One we seek*
*to limn, Whose being lies beyond surmise,*
*uncircumscribed by skin of pearl or dusk,*

*or gaze akin to hue of sky or sea.*
*Let us forsake accustomed shores, incline*
*our sails to harvest winds that hymn the Source*
*Who animates all things by thought alone…*

Nor did transcendence glimpsed abate its trace
through myriad coasts and grim enslavement,
or while his two frail hands delved earth, and tears
consigned two sons to the abiding night.

**Letter from Tarsus**
(28 A.D.)

With all respect to Athenodorus,
a sojourn in this Cilician town is
quite worthless. The locals aim to impress
with grace, but prattle like those honking swans

that glut the Cydnus, whose filthy currents
breed a sultry atmosphere, and appall
even the thirsty. Rituals entice
expectant souls, for the common people

worship a god who rides a horned lion
with wings, and bears in one hand a blossom,
in the other an axe. When he is slain
each spring in effigy, the flames assume

him into heaven, and his sacrifice
brings rain, prosperity and health; some claim
no god yet possessed a lovelier face.
But our citizens from Jerusalem

shun such practices, viewing as impure
what they condemn as idols, obstinate
in their perverse beliefs; yet the Empire
enjoys their loyalty, and their intent

seems without malice. The worst offenders
are those who style themselves philosophers,
and will argue trifling points with wondrous
learning, which they glibly recite for us.

They regard their dismal academy
as rivaling those of Carthage, Corinth
or Antioch, though their love of wisdom
pales beside a zeal for linen (beneath

which their limbs cannot compare with Roman
flesh). Foreigners rarely attend the school,
and natives of promise never remain,
fortune and ambition being fickle.

True, the palaces—for a provincial
capital—boast fine proportions, fountains
sweeten the lanes. Yet its wealth is a shell,
hollowed out by conventions and routines.

Little has changed since Cicero languished
here. Weariness, when evening erases
the sun, is a burden we cannot shed.
Nothing good will ever come of Tarsus.

## Encounter with Asterion

*for Charles Cameron*

*... on high, the intricate sun;*
*on earth, Asterion.*
—J.L. Borges

The fine-grained stone beneath your tread: a map
of vanquished realms, or constellations yet
unknown? *Why speculate*? Though flesh is damp,
your aweless heart conceives no thought of flight;

for now, these walls are world: you grasp that thread
the cunning princess coiled into a skein
the Fates had measured to befit your pride.
*Let prowess ravel out their wry cocoon*!

She'd warned of convolutions, passages
awhirl with flame, of spiraled corridors—
but not the ledge, the vertigo: those jaws
that jut from seething tides no vessel dares

approach. Yet soon the narrow pavement turned
again within: entanglements of stone
gave way to temple, halls unfurled a frond
of paths. Confusion fled: you *would* attain

the victory. You sought the furthest court,
beheld the splay of sunlight where he lay.
His fragrance ravished: that famed stench of rot
was figment. No growl defied, no reply

opposed your threat, nor did he rise. Your thrust
was deft and pitiless. No savage roar
emerged, no spate of gore escaped his breast;
what seeped from flaccid lips resembled prayer.

You'll have no choice but to concoct a foul
detail or two, contrive a rampant brute
and grievous peril. Fable must fulfill
conviction: these amber horns oozing bright

perfume are too sublime to sate the blood.
His beauty shines, belies the tales we've told.
At last you fear, defeated by your deed,
aware too late that you have slain a god.

## Tomb of a Carthaginian Priestess

The bones of one hand encircle still a bronze
mirror; about her desiccated wrist
a bracelet of scarabs, pearls and figurines
sustained the soul whose body death embraced.

At her absent throat, forty pieces of gold
flank a disc of jacinth bearing a turquoise
crescent, alliance of sun and moon sealed
within the solitude where flesh decays.

And we who violate her dark devour
what we bring to light, assess the enamel
flask, collect the ivory and silver.
The living knew her otherwise: a smile

or gesture hinting at a realm so rich
that liturgy might even mask or hinder
its allure. Disdaining our ambitious breach,
her skull stares forth, beyond the eastern door.

## Phidias in Olympia
(433 BC)

*Do not believe*
*only what you see.*
—Cavafy

We cannot conceive what he must have glimpsed
when, abandoning the mortal confines
of his mind, that presence before him passed
beyond all previous theophanies.

The common dome of sky became temple,
serenity's depths encompassed him, huge
and dreadful: by what cunning skill or spell
might he echo divinity's image?

Even Athena's grace had not haunted
him so profoundly, nor had fame prepared
him for this task: to give such plenitude
true form required a sacrifice of pride

he feared long custom placed beyond his reach,
so readily had good things come to hand:
his boyhood flute, his deft gestures, the rich
curve of fruits or covert clefts among nude

limbs he once caressed. Yet all that was lost
now. Far from home, alone with the sacred,
he must humbly begin to elicit
an awesome dignity from nature's crude

gifts: gold's glimmer and polished ivory
were but simulacra, modalities
of dust that mocked his desire to portray
the pure origin of earth's poor delights.

The rogue who accused him of embezzling
gold from the statue of the Parthenos
could not grasp this, of course: such men belong
to that crowd who gladly ruin Athens

for a scrap of glory or feigned applause,
worshipping hollow figments of power
while speaking of honor, praise the polis
as they goad Sparta into bitter war.

Let fools blather of his fabulous wealth
or dismiss him as a propagandist
for Pericles – they could not taste the blithe
rapture that came when matter incandesced,

and a god took shape beneath his fingers.
Poor Pericles! Ambition overruled
him… he spurned even Anaxagoras,
who taught him how the order of the world

left no room for chance… Perhaps he learned this,
yet construes it as the philosopher
did not intend. So here Phidias breathes
more easily than at home, without fear:

he prefers the groves and hills of Elis,
that spot near the shrine of Endymion,
who brought his Aeolians to the place
where his deathless beauty seduced the moon.

And in holy Olympia plane trees
answer the two rivers, temper his toil

until from workmen's hands begins to rise
beyond mutable flesh, above the stale

designs of men, the fair divinity
he dreamt, seated on a throne of cedar
adorned with figures that render finite
his ineffable essence, and adore

the Lord of Time: in ebony and gems
wrought with gold, swarm in a circle of praise
lion and sphinx, Hephaestus and Hermes,
turning Seasons and dancing Victories,

heroes' deeds and victims, life's manifest
ardor and disorder, harmonious
journeys of sun and stars, each a facet
of him, sustained in majestic balance.

His gilded mantle blossoms with lilies
the sculptor's patient nephew Panainos
embroiders in pigment, with animals
that seem to breathe. And last, the face ripens

at the brush's touch, brims with eerie warmth,
a repose in eyes and mouth not aloof
or indifferent to earth, as vulgar myth
tells, but tender: as though within himself

he bore a secret loss that none might share.
On the sultry day when work was finished,
Phidias thought he heard the distant shore
draw near, stir the poplars' merciful shade

about his feet: yet no breeze moved beneath
a stinging sun; three youths lounged by an oak
and talked of ships that had sailed for Corinth.
This brief illusion provoked no panic

or distress, but rather served to remind
him that despite a life spent in avid
pursuit, his craft had ever been summoned
to a perfect beauty no man achieved.

Yet on screens that shield the god from mundane
intrusions, his nephew painted defeats
and trials: alongside Atlas' burden,
the Amazons' doomed queen, Troy's prophetess,

as well as the singing Hesperides.
For the Father sees and embraces all.
And soon pilgrims flock down the dusty roads
to approach the temple with trembling zeal

and pass through those fluted sunlit columns
into torchlight. Even those who believe
but in part, shiver or weep when he looms
above them, feel their griefs and woes dissolve

as they pour oblations of olive oil
that brim the black tiles rimmed with Parian
marble, praying they be kept from evil.
As Phidias will be spared the ruin

of benign Meilichíos… Horkios
Lord of Oaths… Xenios friend of strangers:
refuge from intrigue, outrage and chaos,
whose just wisdom requites all injuries.

Though we're left nothing but a tarnished cup
found, not so long ago, in the remains
of a Byzantine church where his workshop
stood for a time, austere and luminous.

## Leopardi

(1798-1837)
*...nascere al pianto...*

Despair was but the fruit of suffering,
his critics held, and bitter loss in love's
elusive game: not courage but distress
engendered verses ominous and fierce.

And yet he knew he shared the common lot,
the ancient ill which has no remedy,
that tyranny against which we contend
in vain, responding to a noble need:

enslavement to necessity and fate—
which many men deny with platitudes,
concocting craven tales of providence—
while victory lies only in defiance.

Man raises temples, offers sacrifice
and prayer; the gods requite us with disdain,
delight in our misfortune and defeat,
and pity us, audacious and bereft.

Therefore we curse the urns of Zeus—whose mouths
bestrew both good and evil, random gifts,
unmerited prestige and cruel rewards.
Though hopeless, we refuse our destiny,

scorn empty consolation in the thought:
*Our putrid progeny will honor us...*
This vulgar age is nothing but a tomb

for Glory: we blaspheme who speak its name,

as those who perish serve a cunning honor,
surrender strength and beauty to a phantom,
while moon and stone remain to mock soul's breath,
oblivious to misery and death.

Yet visionaries still seek out the rhyme
amid misfortune's measure, time's contempt:
their magnanimity as obstinate
as our inexorable doom is clear.

Those gleanings of the infinite... Divine
unceasing calm... are but amusing toys,
a child's absurd imaginings we scrawl
upon the bleak expanse of nothingness.

Take courage, and renounce worn fantasies:
we are not citizens, but orphans all,
belonging only to that country where
Achilles weeps with Priam in the dark.

## Scorpion

*I am the one confined in fire...*
—Nikos Karouzos

*...Whose venom never yet was vain...*
—Byron

Consuming flames draw nearer still: the smoke
no longer veil or smudge but clots of grime
convolving. Billows clutch at stones, and mock
the frantic will—let other creatures scream

and vainly strive to flee. My carapace
would not protect me, should I writhe or rush;
conserving dignity, I conjure peace.
For death is certain, though I shall not perish.

My forms are myriad; nor time nor place
constrains. Assassin of Orion, friend
of Isis, keeper of that solar threshold
mortals profane to find their hopes denied.

For me the gate lies always open. Fearless,
my loyal barb anticipates the flood
of fire. I need not gasp for breath: the hidden
road of sunrise celebrates its guardian.

## Darkling
(*Eleodes Obscurus*)

*...un ami des ténèbres...*

I must admit the fear,
first hearing it.
That spectral scratching in
sporadic gasps
almost articulate –
hollow whisper
at once erased: my den
an eerie space.

Too faint to be gnawing
mouse in wainscot,
this cramped trace of a hiss
some pensive snake
might let escape (until
the strike or flight)
dispels my scrawling thoughts.
Prickling my neck,

qualms linger still across
the hall, where sleep
begrudges fitful rest.
Two midnights pass
before the delicate
dismay dissolves,
becomes exact in form:
a blot that limps

toward freedom, an oval
obduracy
astray indoors, genus
*Eleodes.*
The Greek is apt: a smooth
shell, olive-like,
is waddling toward the door.
A silence plods

into the dark he seeks,
a night that rhymes
with ebony and ink
of carapace
whose satin varnish fused
two futile wings,
depriving him of flight,
conferring peace

in crevices and gaps.
So I oblige,
and fetch an envelope,
an ample glass.
As I stoop down he ducks
his head and tilts
his abdomen, to mount
superfluous

defense, conjecturing
my fierce intent—
that like grasshopper mice
or scorpions
I plan to feast on him.
The rim descends
to form a lantern where
no flame ripens,

though his black seed of fire

remains aslant
as he is borne beyond
the garden steps,
dropped amid the ivy,
never flinching,
while from the empty glass
pours fetid spice:

a pungent reek belies
the name "clown bug".
(*A forest ranger plucked*
*one off his map,*
*wiped his moustache and watched*
*the world double:*
*staggering, he took two*
*hours to reach camp.*)

I find nothing comic
in this beetle's
pose. Mythic roots incline
him; curious
accounts construe his stance,
its origins
in hapless negligence
or clever ruse.

Cochiti legend tells
that he first dipped
his head in shame, because
he spilled the stars;
the Zuni say he slipped
Coyote's jaws
by feigning to perceive
the mysteries

the gods were murmuring
beneath the earth.

Trickster, *tenebrio*:
a night spirit
haunting murky places,
detritivore
whose body of shadows
thrives upon rot.

A mountain range recalls
his Aztec name–
*Pinacate*: black rock
and cinder cones,
craters, smugglers' haven,
barren Altar:
aeolian sands, star
and crescent dunes.

But here among the leaves
fragility
prevails, a compact pause
slowly recedes,
swaying into dappled
damp of autumn,
obscure again beneath
the Pleiades.

## The Count

*...ton esclavage maudit...*
—Baudelaire

In all the volumes fraught with legend, folklore
and history devoted to him, we learn
the signs: rapacious flesh bereft of color,
a form the mirror shuns, his visage forlorn
yet merciless. A votary of blood,
he curses every hour of his immortal
existence, craving nothing but the fabled
death that never comes to finish the tale.

Of this both lunatics and scholars fail
to speak: the inner torment of that soul
who once imagined something beautiful
and stronger than his will would storm the castle
to make him like other men—small and banal,
content with change, uncertainty, renewal.

## A Notebook of 1920

*Ici commence l'indecible...*
—Rilke

Familiar lanes and streets you had not seen
since that August when the world succumbed to hate
reach out, enfold you. Along the Rue de Seine
you pause beside a modest window where white

lace filigrees the light's descent; the reek
of cheap tobacco permeates a threshold
whose door allows a glimpse of tattered fabric.
And all at once your ruptured heart is healed:

the gardens have not vanished, the river braids
its ageless waters. Everything you seek
already is: a shabby paradise
made visible in bakery and kiosk;

faces your mind had fossilized bestow
their ripened forms. The blind man on the bridge
for whom you feared the winter of 1902
abides the rain, and contemplates the verge

of holy patience he still yearns to cross.
Amid the crowd you glimpse the same cravat,
a mouth transfigured by sublime distress;
waifs and bankers, prostitutes and nuns invite

your memory to enter that pavilion
where frozen figures pullulate, and dazzle
the disciple, while the Master works alone,
shaping realms of rhythm with his chisel.

The city you detested sates your eyes,
and in your notebook spawns a precious seed:
before the void of leaves begins, you praise
that universe of what cannot be said.

## Seventy Years

*John Jacob Ruster*
*(1913-1995)*

In a grove
            you resemble
the other trees,
yet you teach them
to change:
            to become doors,
to unfurl fire.

In the earth
            you traced
furrowed runes
that articulated stems
and petals:
            your toil
recited gardens.

Your embrace
            widened
until your hands
forgot each other,
imagined themselves
                  wings,
and flew through the world.

Father,
      you have seen

so much that your eyes
                    are naked
from having
          opened places
others never named.

## True Tongue

All through childhood I never lied:
how could I possibly dare try?
Cats and dogs spoke to me aloud;

my sage older brother could fly
almost to the face of the moon
(as far, at least, as Italy);

my mother's fresh hands of jasmine
would heal even lepers, for she
was no ordinary woman;

and my father's gaze, acutely
honed, knew every shape in the world,
save the goblins in the pear tree

where I might settle on some gnarled
branch to ponder whether horses
sleep with wings folded or unfurled.

I learned how the spring sun raises
the dead from mire to leaf: sure sign
that Christ lay curled in the grasses.

My tongue could find no cause to sin:
What need had I to gild lilies,
in a realm beyond invention
where truth outstripped the boldest lies?

## A Lemon

In each of my gardens there were lemons:
as if, unwittingly, I've followed some
secret path marked by these bitter omens –
yet where it might lead I won't dare presume,

unable to read the constellations
whose light has sifted down through waxen leaves
to haunt me thus, and prepare my patience
for the long journey of sorrows and loves.

Scores of them have laced my tea, spiced my soup,
diverse in form as any eye could ask,
though never so singular as the shape
my careless hand plucked last night after dusk:

by a most curious geometry
sadly misshapen, not remotely round
nor yet graced with pleasing asymmetry,
but insect-pocked, a bulbous parchment rind.

Still, I harbor no pity toward this fruit:
for out of the seething mineral loam,
from pungent marriage of pollen and rot,
through labyrinths of snarled root and gnarled limb,

the tree, sedulous and joyful, has wrought
– beneath skin my blade pares to sudden flesh –
a prodigy of impeccable art
where fallen filaments of sunlight mesh

with orbits of brilliant wings in a dome
of fragrance that assails and charms the sense.
In its gathered gold I glimpse the wisdom
to seek consolation in bitterness,

to exult in whatever is given.
May we plunge beyond our stains and possess
such beauty: gladly thus endure, even
thrive, under acidulous auspices.

## Invisible Glance

For years he has haunted the same threshold,
begging for a seed of light: an empty
wound where a mind once dwelt, gash never healed
by passing gazes that offered pity

yet withheld the one thing that might embrace
him, sever from shadow and stone a life
stifled by hopes become delirious,
figments that exalt before they engulf.

From that petrified dark his dim eyes still
seek us out, flame faltering for a wick
amid spent wax, final spark of bestial
warmth, foam agleam in a vanishing wake.

## With No Abode

*for Daniel Wasserman*

*...between Elim and Sinai...*
—Exodus 16:1
*...confirming what is with them...*
– al-Bakarah (2:)91

Through brutal sands we traipse, alone.
Do not beg for manna or quail,
disdain the allure of the calf,
nor disbelieve what lies beyond.
Forget what you once feigned to need.
Forgive the souls who groan and scoff...
but breathe upon the waning coal,
revere the prophets we have slain.

## Tabor

*...Surgite, et nolite timere...*
—Mt. 17:7

### I. *Anabasis*

Not asking what he meant to accomplish,
we staggered through shadow—you know the slopes,
how steep and strewn the path. The dome of night
embraced the crest. We saw his form remain
while gleam of phosphor swelled to glory: moon
and sun commingled there; music and scent
were wed. Might fear not flare yet soon collapse,
beholding Mystery inscribed in flesh?

### II. *Katabasis*

We dare not hope to comprehend that glimpse,
or grasp that such splendor should come before
scandal. We descend to face our return
to daily toil and trial, to stench and strife,
and shun no stranger's sorrow. Although grief
may snare our steps, this night a veil was torn:
our taints became tincture, our frailty fire,
our silence a realm no words encompass.

## The Vacant Cross

*for Gaza, for Syria, for Yemen*

*...what men do not see they easily forget...*
—St. François de Sales

Such comfort in that burnished, empty Cross,
its gleam of hope and peace: no hint of wound
or agony, no paradox of Grace
and misery sublimely intertwined.
Reminders of fragility distress
us, dim the happiness we must defend
from dismal images that feed morose
ideas, lest faith be daunted or profaned.

Once, and for all time, our sins were lifted—
why dwell on distant wars, on mothers' wombs
defiled, mazes of dust where houses stood,
where fathers cradle daughters' shattered limbs?
Our thoughts and prayers will heal, the horrors fade...
And none dare claim they have been crucified.

## Easter Vigil
*(Sábado de Gloria)*

*for Elizabeth*

*Il y a un autre monde mais il est dans celui-ci.*
—Paul Eluard

A sky composed of pearl, parabolas
and veins of ash, soft blush of violet.
You pause to gaze, murmur: "*As if Mozart*
*had leapt into the air and painted this...*"
Yes: felicity with wistful pathos
mingles, transcendence and transience consort.
Though sun declines, the soul discovers flight,
embracing every moment that we lose.

## Carved Virgin

*(St. Stephan, Mainz)*

*She, wild web, wondrous robe...*
—G.M. Hopkins

The flames have gathered at her feet like eyes,
and within her flaring robe, hooded souls
look up, cheeks burnished in the fragrant glow.
Smooth grain tapers, curves, contracts to pure gaze,
that she might glimpse, through shabby lives, vessels
filled with holy purpose, astray below.

She remains in rapturous colloquy
with all; our fervor to be made entire
is her own first hope, and who hears earth mourn
but one who encircles both sea and sky?:
wave of cresting fire, star sculpting a tear,
abiding balm of the lost and forlorn.

# Eros / Algos

*Where love, there pain.*
—Kathleen Raine

## Apotheosis of Earthly Love

Here below, thick shadows flicker, like fire
consumed by its fury to writhing ash.
The steps are damp; you breathe stifling sulphur,
your mind repels distant howls of anguish.

Deeper, where the path borders a crevasse,
you stand before the Lords of this bleak realm,
and humbly lift the lyre, your vibrant voice
lapping somber ears, caressing the gloom

that swarms, coils in stagnant vaults and hollows.
And harmonies that stunned beasts and quickened
trees to rejoice melt death's obdurate laws
and render Hades' abysmal heart kind:
for your soul is ravished by a goddess,
though you sing of mortal Eurydice.

## Surrender

### I. The Poet

We hear there is a garden that invites
us to serenity. A sublime pool
deeper than sorrow, where the covetous
might purge their wounds of yearning, a temple
immune to siege, quake or time – illumined
from within – adorn its lofty center,
where moonlight sheds the fragrance of almond,
rapture revives our innocence entire.
Yet here our days are fierce winds, wild oceans;
and as that gate is shut until our lives
wilt, we bear and celebrate our passions.
Lord, haven frail souls; save us from ourselves,
deliver us from languorous fevers:
for what we embrace cannot devour us.

### II. The Contemplative

See how mystery enfolds us, dissolves
the will's grasping heat, lest we learn too late
that water mingled with mirage enslaves
beyond sheer illusion's ghostly delight.
It's true that we were made for fire. Bright threads
pierce and span our being, though still we fail
to discern the dim gate of paradise:
in our thirst for yet more dazzling fuel,
we blithely invite longing to benight
the heart, convert flesh to raging furnace –
though even now we touch the Infinite,
and bear both stars and oceans within us.
On each breath a fragile moment dilates
and we are ravished beyond all frailties.

## A Moment Fastened

*for Myrna*

Once my face dissolves, you may not recall
the grief that stained whatever light dwelt there:
stillborn joys, vestiges of ridicule,
remorseful murk of the soul's foul weather.

The failures of my hands you shall forget:
melodies never caressed, unmended
shards in cupboards, hasp of a promised gate
where rust blooms under vines that surged and died.

Only two or three things bear remembrance
when all the ferments of our years have staled.
Once, as you turned, my words dared to resume
their source: we felt ocean's breast blaze to bronze,
and hungered for myths that could not be told,
our ache a net that spanned the heart's chasm.

## Aubade

Morning sealed still under night's final pulse.
Soul, do not rise into that waking dark
our habit calls life: grim metropolis
of bastard fact and political trick

whose every color resembles the bruise
of limp compassion stifled by demand,
until we navigate our miseries
with ease, wings being severed from the mind.

Linger yet, my soul, in this translucence
of sleep, your sighs with seas interwoven,
bones of moon's mineral light, sinuous
blood ripening into gems on the vine.

Let me forget my fire has diminished,
have me believe how water can be brought
to birth, though I fail to love as I should
on this earth where shadows reverberate.

## Concourse

Even now, embraced
                    by a tenuous morning,
the horse on the beach
is still the color of moon.

In the east, a stairway of light,
diaphanous cataract:
                    the transparent present.
Among knotted paths,
                    wind unfastens
the scorched constellations
of fallen leaves.

We walk through the murmur
of a passionate sea:
vast lace of nuptial hands.
                    Our tongues
exchange brine.
            Our souls
are composed of sand.
                    Behind us,
shadow carves resonance
in our footsteps.

All the shut gates
            have dissolved.
The doorways
            are dust.
Inchoate architecture:
                    the air

is a vociferous menagerie of wings.

When night descends
you will become
                    that infinite rose
engulfing my being.

## Waiting

*for Myrna*

Scarcely changed by day's slow retreat, our house
retains the image that met your last glance:
letters like questions flung open, some loose
coins, an orphan shoe, the taciturn plants.

My thoughts and gestures have peopled the room
with ghosts that now redouble your absence,
threatening to engulf my vague tasks in grim
anonymity and troubled silence.

Darkness unravels, the cries of birds fray
into stillness that augurs no repose
under glum heavens wearily unfurled.

Why are my limbs and eyes reduced to clay
without your gaze to caress and oppose?
How can your mere hands awaken a world?

## Nuptials

*for Charles and Anne*

*The world of nature consists*
*of... a single form, reflected*
*in many mirrors.*
—ibn 'Arabi

Who would dare cleave translucence from crystal,
or sunder purple from the swelling plum?
Can music from sound unwind her subtle
mesh, or fragrance be sifted from the bloom?

Ocean and its tide of tongues are woven
into one brocade; sky weds light with heat;
mild fields, wild forests lace earth to heaven;
webbed nebulae couple chasm and height.

So do lovers to such fusion aspire.
May the vast realm of knitted things forbid
all harm or chance to separate this pair:
for sun and moon shall mingle in their bed.

## Ecstasy

Light.

Cycles of light.

Synergy of water and light:
                                        opalescence
that enchants
with the frailty of fingers,
splendor
              curving

through the vessel you indwell.

Sheer life
              given shape,
you embody
                   resonance
made substance:
                        modulating
within a firm skin,
                           you deliquesce,
your bones mingling
                              before resuming
their solidity:
                    you flow
to the limits of your form.
                                    Released,
you besiege the contours
that caress you,
hazard the effacement

of your symmetry
in that same cataract of life
which awakens music
from the stone.

I leave myself,
unbolt
the windows of my eyes:
embracing you,

I disembody my body,
advance into the wind's body.

In the repletion
of noon,
I plunge
into the night of your hips,
nocturnal river
carving its figure in space,
river that flows,
that changes
and remains changeless,
current
dispersing itself
into the breast
of day:
translucency
springing
from a perilous congruence
of gardens:
eternity
stilled
in the moment.

## Winter Consolation

A few curled leaves cling where wind failed to tear
them from limbs autumn left briefly richer,
as scent still lingers in the chill sweater
a lover cast off in an empty chair.

*

## What Remained

A final garment of the light dissolves
till silhouettes of boughs unite with sky.
From someone far away a sigh escapes
—or did the sorrow drift from one of us?

We never mention what we failed to find
as fingers delve in pocket for a key.
Before your hand can reach the lamp, we glimpse
the trace of phosphorescence left behind.

## Cleft and Clasp

*A Retort*

*But 'twas beyond a mortal's share*
*To wander solitary there:*
*Two paradises 'twere in one*
*To live in Paradise alone.*
– Andrew Marvell

You are mistaken, Andrew: solitude
is no finer state. Your dream of benign
garlands, herbs, and perfumes unpolluted
is delusion, without a companion.

What marvel could endure in a garden
bereft of woman? Call it paradise,
while the lavish slopes turn to barren dune,
sterile soil usurps the loam. You reduce

the consanguinity of moon and sun
to grit, God's conjunctions to a trifle;
trample rich vineyards for a lone raisin,
cleave Easter's nectar from the fruits of Fall,

and forfeit the harvest of a soul shared,
when the dove's wings clasp in the maid's orchard.

## Ode to the Letter V

Its figure intimates a downward veer,
a swift descent, abrupt collapse or fall
that varies with what view we choose to favor:
a moral failure, or a loss of fuel.

Yet if we pause to hear... she marks a drift
diverging from her voiceless, puffing twin,
who finds his fate in flute and flood, defeat
and feeble flesh. Though pointing glumly down,

this wedge of ink invites the voice and breath
to merge, while tooth and lip converge to yield
an interval amid the wanton growth
of vowels, consonants whose bones collide,

while sibilants that sputter sex and zest
succumb with surly zeal to liquids' lure.
By contrast, *v* invokes a lover's visit:
arrival, verge, unveiling, avid flare

of reverence mere craving would evict.
That simple groove is vibrant vesicle,
where seeds of silence learn to advocate
the hum and harmony of things, recall

the soul from vestige to divinity:
discovering each curve, elusive crevice,
aroma's evanescence, as event
within the weave of an eternal voice

that savors leaves and evening, brevities

voluptuous and vulnerable; havens
what ravels, hovers, vanishes; devotes
itself to visions, aviaries, vines.

But nor does it avoid ambivalence
or evil: motives we deceive ourselves
we never served, invented villainies
of others, vanities that make us slaves

to rivalry and waving flags. Naïve
and clever victims, we call vengeance brave,
revile those thieves we envy, then connive
to vindicate our vice. And if we grieve

when heaviness invades our net of veins,
we contravene the void it carves, ensnare
a lenitive in striving to convince
with drivel and a frivolous veneer,

like strangers to privation or divorce,
travail of childbirth, invalid's decline.
While *v*, receptively omnivorous,
avails the virus, glove or violin.

Perhaps it quivers in the name of Devil,
disavowing his devices and covens,
conveys Avernus' murk but to reveal
and elevate the fervent gleam of Venus,

observes with us the seven days Mosaic
Law, severe and benevolent, ordains
for mourning, even there preserving music
plaintive yet unvanquished, sliver of the dance

that Pārvatī and Shiva consecrate.
As worlds evolve, dissolve, revive, Tāndava
envelops all division: indiscrete,

the universe convulses in the dove.

Our lives are involutions, vortices
we scarce perceive. Although evasions thrive,
vitality prevails, pervading tissues
of the visible with what we cannot prove.

And thus, this letter's volume is penumbral,
provoking meditative minds to delve
beneath the lovely surface of the real,
where Virgin, convolvulus, velvet, vulva

engrave upon imagination's heaven
a cove inviolate, a vale our travels
never reach, where havoc might not intervene
between our vision and the marvelous.

## Remnants

It's only natural we should resent
the small or great betrayals of our love:
the silent scorn or bitter word does not
inflict a petty wound that smiles might solve.

It's understandable we fear the end
has come, once emptiness and pain prevail:
to find unspoken hint and subtle nod
usurped by glaring looks where demons prowl.

One last unbroken thread remains, before
the dreaded banishment of soul from soul:
let neither dare to feign the embers' warmth
has fled, though long ago we passed through fire,
when tide and myth still beckoned us to sail,
your body's melody upon my mouth.

## Cunnilingus

*Mi lengua de sol en tu bosque...*
*Tu cuerpo en mi cuerpo...*
—Octavio Paz

But shun the clinical array
of terms or euphemisms used
in prim evasion; banish all
the vile irreverence a tongue
might shape: let its inflections curve
and flutter as its wings arrive
on tuft and petal, taste the sting
of ocean's nectar in that shell
where feather, frond and sap reside;
caress and delve until the cry
blends moan and praise, encompassing
fragility with ardent song.

## Presages

How suddenly the light
                                        can change,
withdrawing from your cheek
those trembling webs of burnt
                                                orange
that hovered on the lake.

How fiercely wind erodes
                                            our words,
snatching frail syllables
to feed the gasping mouths
                                            of reeds
where no remembrance blows.

How anxiously I sought
                                        your hand,
our gathered fingers cold
as earth when dawn
lies cramped
                    behind
steep labyrinths of cloud.

We dare not linger till
                                    the owls
arise
        to clasp their night,

but wander home
                    through brooding hills,
in dread and ardor knit.

## An Old Greek Nun Recalls Her Youth

I never thought to spend my life alone.
On many nights my fingers conjured hands
that never grazed this curve, that secret moss
whose dampness Yannis (no doubt Nikos, too)
imagined, trembling, when he dreamt my shape.

One midnight, near the end of June,
I stood before the mirror, nude. In light
the candle scarcely whispered, I invoked
St. John, then slept content with ancient lore:
the name next heard would be my destined mate.

My father rarely swore. And yet, before
the dawn had touched one starling's folded wing,
he stumbled on the stairs, and roused the house
with curses meant for Heaven's ear, not mine.
And so it was: his oath became my vow.

I told the abbess once, disclosing all
my sins, those fantasies I entertained
so long ago, but she's forgotten now.
And since my ripeness faded, other joys
I'd not envisioned mellowed in their place:

monastic toil, perpetual repose,
the delicate incision prayer performs,
that one might taste the love which only comes
when nothing is expected in return,
our flesh a threshold of the infinite.

## Before the Summer

*for AAM*

*Beautiful, fragile, fleeting...*
*but not, for all that, illusory.*
—Anne Morrow Lindbergh

Before the summer has flown you will turn
with tender gloom to cross the road one last
time; pause as you enter the strange terrain
of solitude, not a wild bird released
in the dawn, but a child expelled from home,
foreseeing even now the cherished place
become ghostly, as the retreating hem
of daylight dissolves in the dusk of loss.

Before the summer began you were called
to delight—finches drenching sycamores
in song, whispers rich with wine—and were glad
to caress the promise of memories,
abide both bud and thorn, seek nothing more
than communions fragile as gossamer.

## Renovation

*for MRV*

I hope we might see each other again.
Our gazes would converge in a single
flame that once extinguished would not be gone,
but linger in the eye, like a seagull
veering out of sight, yet ever rising
on the early air's invisible spire.

Perhaps that ancient tune the blind man sang
in Veracruz, before we knew despair,
might haunt us once more, or the lavender
of Oregon return inviolate.

And your voice would be laced with the candor
of a planet emerging from twilight
in the freshly wakened wind of autumn,
where we unfold our souls for the first time.

## *Tenebrae*

You cannot reach me now. We are sealed off,
two spirits pent in regions of our own
where we stammer and cry before the deaf
gate, stagger blind in a bone-bound ruin,

forgetting how the tongue of a candle
could sing a sphere of brightness in the murk
or scant breeze mingle with the crush of dill,
and fresh dawn's dazzled clouds of turmeric

dissolve in one serene pool of sapphire.
Yet by now the wind bears only the scent
of fear, and life without light is safer,
though here and there, some still hallucinate:

question how many realms we dare erase,
and hearing the voice of our enemies,
a hand begins to shape a shy caress,
lips again utter the intimate names.

## Incarnation: A Gloss

(Gregory of Nyssa,
*Life of Moses*, II.201, 256)

The first to deem corrupt the sight of flesh
unclad were no doubt dazzled and confused
by that glory; and ever since, foolish
tongues have pronounced anathema when faced
with a display of secret skin, one glimpse
of which kindles the blood's benighted lamps.

Yet the bare form enciphers a riddle:
see those roughhewn feet humbly kiss the earth,
while lathed pillars converge in a cradle
of fire? How the breast exults in its girth,
and eyes pour forth the wonders that circle
in the dark vaulted cosmos of the skull!

Did ever landscape more amaze than these
realms of nacre, amber, clove and sable
that splendour the trunk from shoulders to thighs?
Apotheosis of the visible,
emblem of the unseen, more dangerous
than opium, more sacred than the rose.

How could one contemplate this frame and see
no marvel, but a presage of the tomb
and ample reason to lament and sigh?
The crown of silk, the nether meadow's thyme
and sage suffice to clothe; nor might a shroud
sublime what heaven sent without a shred.

Let sun caress, rain bless, the vales and slopes
of skin tender as a ripe persimmon:
shape divinely wrought, free of stain or lapse.
What else did Gregory of Nyssa mean
by that phrase? – "Unless thy foot be unshod,
thou canst not ascend the mountain of God."

## Nocturnal Flight

And so I fall asleep between your arms,
once more delivered from the hourly death
of staggering blind through palpable dreams:
borne up toward fragrant landscapes on your breath.

*

## Again...

And yet in spite
of all, you still
possess the power
to break my heart.

Once more the dream,
that precious gaze;
the hollow word,
the silenced scream.

## Palimpsest

*...so that I could hold it there forever.*
—AAM

Upon white dunes
you once inscribed
*Forever*: grains
a photograph preserves.

Could it be true
that every word
was marvelous,
and every gesture blessed,

our litanies
a dance, a gaze
engraved with tears
that echoed galaxies?

You guided me
into your depths,
where oceans sang
and shadows blazed with fruit.

Our life deferred
spanned years alone,
though distances
did not efface the hope

nor quarrels curse
the destiny
communion traced—
until at last lives merged.

Should we have glimpsed
the bitterness
of paradise,
foreseen the vanished vows,

heard fresh music
molder, smelled lost
scent arising
from a vacant mirror?

Yet never guessed
an arctic stare
might cleave my soul,
a heartless voice destroy

the worlds we shaped
with holy tongues,
or reverence
beget banality,

the agony
inaudible
above the bleak
oblivion you wove,

not having meant
to poison us
with promises
forever unredeemed.

## Ruthless Ardor

In the end, there's but a lonely reason
why a mouth that once melted with your own
should seethe and ignite in acts of arson,
rendering your frame a gutted ruin,

for beneath the rages that enumerate
your every terrible or trifling deed
abides a failure to foresee regret,
or recall how no fire attends the dead.

# Lachrimæ Rerum

*Sunt lacrimae rerum*
*et mentem mortalia tangunt.*
—Virgil

## Undisclosed:
*A Plea for Melancholy*

*...un crépuscule...*
*une sombre joie.*
—Victor Hugo

Speak the truth. Despite companions
by the score, stray pleasures tempered
by restraint and purpose, demons
duly tamed, scintillas of joy—
within us broods an elegy
we fear to sing, whose ominous
profundity no soul is spared,
whose holy gloom no cheer profanes.

## Hidden Bounty

*What you resist persists.*
—*attrib.* C.G. Jung

A tangled task. To stoop and heave, with arms
and shoulders thrusting deep into the dark
accumulation: shadows filling rooms
where still you shovel griefs, as if to break

the spell they cast, efface them from your gaze.
They swell the cupboards, cram the cellar: heaps
of anguish you long labored to disguise,
lost questions, false reprieves that stifle peace,

and remedies you never dared to risk.
They cling to you, more obstinate than dust,
companions you would eagerly forsake,
imagining the wounds might be reduced.

You toil in vain. Grant shelter—do not shift
or flee those ancient sorrows that beset
you: they conceal the harvest of defeat
whose pungent ripeness bears the gift you sought.

## A Daughter's Kite

*for Sofía*

Return, my love, my child: that pristine shore
awaits us yet, where shipwrecked winds dispel
our sorrow, muster what remains to share.
Unwrap the flaunting fabric, raise the spool

and let the string unwind; relent your grip
a little, making hands a nest for pulse
and faith, a tacit melody grown ripe
as tautness gathers in the twine. Release

that seed of color in the womb of light,
inflect unsullied blue with lilting sail
or petal's dance, untangle and dilate
the spark that lingers in a dusky soul,

as if I lifted you again upon
once steadfast shoulders, holding you aloft,
your fingers grazing realms bereft of pain,
until we reach the place we never left.

## Familiar Faces

*Her mother's face is so familiar*
*that she can't see her.*
—Debra Dean

You strive to summon the unique shade of
sapphire or coffee gracing the center
of that eye, or the small swell of a dove
nestling beside each nostril. The entire
curve caressing forehead or chin may rise
to mind, yet not those cheeks' peculiar sheen.

Our memory's version of Cassandra's
curse: knowledge deprived of recollection.

The precious features you desire to bless
with permanence elude you like the shape
of a shattered glass, until nebulous
contours deny the flesh its fellowship,
though you are joined together still, even
as your own face yields to oblivion.

## November Heaven

Forgive me, sullen sky, for my too glib
desire to seek a refuge from your shroud,
forsaking melancholy's lullaby
of muted light and chill for comfort's fraud.

Your promises are soft—an end to woes,
the sleep of strife—yet we men shy from truth.
Our nature is to wish things otherwise,
a path we chose soon after primal breath

began to flow. Complacency's our fate
by now, escape inscribed upon our flesh.
Delight and ease deceive us: branch bereft
appears an absence only, and that lush

translucency of archipelagoes
—your pulse a maze of pearl and wool in flight—
seems merely pale. Recall and cleanse my gaze:
sift clarity from drifting clouds of slate.

Remind me of that pagan god who grieved
because his loss was deathless. Gently sing
your vision of decline that none evade,
of lives more precious for their perishing.

Let me discern amid your drifts of mist
a void serenity, perhaps a gate
awaiting: regions that elude conceit,
lest I my blessed mortality forget.

## Crepuscular Flock

Though gusts have ceased at last, the sea
is rampant yet.  Of hidden flock
no hint, until a flutter snares
my glance, erupts into a squall
of panting seeds that swarm and sift
in fervid hieroglyphs aloft.
*Resuscitated shadows, quell*
*this torpid anguish that inures*
*me to your signs, dispel the bleak*
*I breathe, revise lament to sigh,*
*and petty prisons where we bask*
*be crucified upon the dusk.*

## A Mother Mourns a Miracle

*for Miriam Cristina Alcántara*

Bring me a vase to bear the ashes home –
let him linger awhile, until the wind
unravels what remains, and earth receives
the echo of that melody of flesh.

Do not dwell on what he *might* accomplish...
those years my cares and prayers could not devise:
yet cherish grace and frailty once entwined
when singing dust was woven in my womb.

## Counsel From An Apparition

*In mem. REB*

When she comes you will not believe,
her face eroded in rest, form
scarcely distinct from a shadow;
when she appears you will murmur
with your fumbling voice, "Pale Mother,
see: I keep you here amid life.

"Since your passage I have honored
you in these: this cup yet bears breath
from your sigh, this spoon I've polished
to the round mirror that wove milk
into your tea, your brush retains
a signature of fragrant hair.

"To conserve the Monet's colors
exactly as you beheld them
I have not gazed upon it once.
No head has dreamed on your pillow."
And threads of a dim voice reply:
"Do morbid relics invoke me?

"I spun my life from quartz and grief,
peopled my deserts with parrots
and harps, kindled stars in men's loins.
Harbor, child, the breeze of my hands,
forgive me obscure caprices;
but dissolve the rest, and be whole."

## Unperishing

(*A daughter's gloss upon a verse of Ursula*)

*I went alone, knowing the gifts' full worth...*
—Ursula Vaughan Williams

*In mem.* Dennis McGregor

Dispersing mourners. Hands and hugs; maudlin
or profound exchanges. Tissues. Ashes...
Then home: I went alone, yet not alone,
burdened with the scent he left, the scarred shoes

so neatly placed, his presence merciless
in blind eyeglasses perching on the shelf.
Encircling me, he joins the other souls
who span the mist I've come to call my life,

this meager nest I shape with open palm
and heart too often half ajar, until
mere tokens of the lost acquire a gleam,
presumed banalities dissolve, and stale

events unfold a precious wake. I hear
a silent step, reply to whispers night
invents, and visit ghostly regions where
our clumsy eschatologies cannot

begin to penetrate. Yet knowing the gifts
at last, I offer up a fervent promise,
replace the lid and shelve the box of photos.
Vanished: nothing now can take him from us,

for blossom has returned beyond its bud,
concealed the measure of a life's full worth
in depths where time and form do not abide.
And trembling into grace, I welcome dearth.

*

## Insatiable

That house beside the sea, its crooked pine
a promise of contentment long withheld.
Unfailing wisdom, fabled silver spoon.
The fine career, angelic spouse, a child

immune to every fashion, lie and wound.
Have you not learned it yet? Our fervent hopes
are only cunning cages for that wind
whose breath conveys the scent of infinite space.

No, yearning and your days will never match,
although your life's a sacred flame in bone.
So let it be enough – however much
you might have craved what almost could have been.
Or else remain, to strive and cling, still avid –
and everything you grasp will bear the void.

## Vespers at Mendocino

The air grows dense with calm, as if a lute
whose themes vexed grass and shivered pines had ceased
to play. From scarred bluffs the heavy twilight
flows, wave blurs with bird: form cannot persist.

A thread of highway remotely unwinds
through wooded slopes; a shipwrecked cloud obscures
the cliff where earth precipitously ends,
briefly haunted by the rare glow of cars.

And motley splendor of midday dissolves
to pallor: sight must surmise a world strewn
with gold and violet blooms, lustrous leaves
enduring only in the mind's terrain.

Such margins of uncertainty prevail
in fugitive light. Each defined surface
yields contour, pattern, texture, to reveal
the dwelling dark, and become amorphous.

Between the huddled cypresses faint wraiths
draw their gowns, somber and ephemeral.
I feel you shift beside me, saying, "This,
no less than light, is the realm of the real."

How true. Near noon the sea lapped quickened jade
against the shoreline's gleaming hide, and that
lone pelican immersed his neck, then plunged
to depths we could not guess, like some vague thought.

They are deceived who say brightness dispels
enigma: though day dazzle the avid
eye, our blind veins trace mystery's dim pulse,
and crave what clarity cannot provide.

## Autumn Nocturne

*...mighty womb of revelations...*
—Novalis

Though it might have been foretold in whispers
plucked from haunted oaks by winds that harvest
prophecies before all hope disappears,
you did not expect that secret visit.

Not your hand but Night herself unfastened
lock and opened up to let the spirit
enter, drift through rooms, and without a sound
find the garden steps, as if to depart

once more, penetrate the dark that nestled
there among the listless ivy, finespun
weeds and summer ghosts. But was it solid
flesh or phantom form that with wistful pain

drew you toward the juniper? Those fragile
fingers lightly grazed your wrist, while voiceless
words invited you to witness the jewel
rising in the eastern sky: a chalice

wrought from light and burnished alabaster
veined with marl; the clouds of clotted nacre
wove an evanescent monastery
—or a glacial reef where sailors anchor

after death—around the sphere's imagined
verge. There stood perfection's emblem obscured:

dusk and luster enlaced, penumbras joined,
contraries covened in a single chord.

Thirst possessed your gaze, until that figure
smiled and touched you yet again, a summons
urging you to sit, converse and linger
still, become an echo of those harmonies,

know yourself as marvel twinned with blemish,
tenebrous splendor, substance made of mist,
timeless pattern impressed on mortal mesh,
world and void condensed within a facet.

Hours elapsed. You spoke of joy and sorrow,
shadow sang to shadow, telling of light
unlost. Though far too soon that guest withdrew
and you were left transformed and incomplete.

## Exile

*Spooner's Cove*

*Aspro è l'esilio...*
—Salvatore Quasimodo

Because I do not live beside the sea
no mist can squander its harvest of tears,
sandstone forgets the form of ecstasy,
arid nights breathe no fragrance of guitars.

Because we do not drowse upon the shore
winds fleeing the sun bring heat without warmth,
horizon is merely earth's erasure,
evening leaves no hint of salt on your mouth.

Because I have abandoned the sacred
tide, sky cannot become a secret shell
where voyages of birds are filigreed
while a wave flings pearls from its unfurled shawl.

Now that we stroll no more along the strand
the cypress does not harbor sweet shadows
that fall like ripe fruit on luminous ground,
and dawn is bereft of mineral dews.

Ocean once embraced us, wrapped its garland
round footprints that had been effaced before;
but we took the long road, and wandered blind
toward solitudes never fraught with sapphire.

## A Garden Regained

*In mem.* Alma Rule Elliott

Those languid summer nights: I remember
how pulsing crickets summoned the twilight
that years later still tastes of the warm beer
sipped, frothless, from my mother's green goblet,

and Grandma, delicate yet casual,
deals cards, as she'll do each night for three weeks,
eyes impish in a face pale as eggshell,
quick hands flecked with raindrops or stains of wax

under seals that flake from old envelopes.
Yet fresh realms opened at their touch: peaches
tinged with dawn's light, a tin filled with lapis
and turquoise, the scarlet rind of smoked cheese,

the elusive secrets of solitaire,
a melon's wondrous heart, sweet and wounded,
the strange music of a faded letter.
She never spoke of when Grandfather died,

but mentioned often the delight she found
in the healing shade of desert willows
strummed as evening's breeze roamed like some orphaned
angel; though when she embraced me, her blouse

would smell of sun. Now that those things are gone,
I can discern the form behind their shapes,
and find the vanished gifts where they began:
in the first garden. Memory worships

what no desire can grasp, nor mind explain,
but glimpses radiance in the simplest
gesture, in a slice of watermelon:
"Always save," she urges, "the heart till last."

## Forever, Ephemeral

*There is nothing as near as the eternal.*
—John O'Donohue

July came far too rarely for a boy
whose father's face endured for but a moon
each year. Yet when that melancholy bay
unfolded, you forgot the pangs of famine.

I often stood within the tide's wild tongue,
while suck of tangling sea devoured each thread
of sand beneath, enraptured at the sting
of danger feigned—as he secreted pride

in pipesmoke prayers that navigated thirst
and gloom with ghosts of laughter. Hours were maps
where all we could not share became erased:
sand and smoke summoned eternity's compass...

He might remain forever kindly wise;
and I, estranged from loss, would never cleave
(once time recurred and brought more careful ways)
to safe restraint, deny undying love.

## A Teardrop

*for Justine Kennedy*

You cannot have noticed the miracle
(brief as it was, and since the eye is blind
to itself): the vibrant force of your gaze
begin to melt and flow, beget a drop
on verge of lid and lash – poise become ripe
translucency. Aslant through curtain's gauze,
sun turned the sphere to gem, until that blend
of soul and fire fell, grace beyond recall.

## Winter Affinity

*...non vanno lontano.*
—Salvatore Quasimodo, "I morti"

A moon astray beyond the stark motif
of ashen cloud; the north wind stings through fleece,
laps at flesh, mocks the refuge of the bone.
At every stone you linger, utter names
whose lives and faces are anonymous,
your own breath unfurling in a ribbon
as wizened branches waver, interlace,
murmur the rhythm of your epitaph.

## Old Ones

And have you seen?—how slowly
the old ones move, with what breadth
their gestures embrace delay:
not as one might deny death

or rehearse a hopeless plea,
but to trace a momentum
whose nature cannot display
itself to those within time.

On the bench, there: that remote
gaze verges on some veiled place,
an expanse more intimate
than flesh with its faithless pulse.
We hasten by, look askance,
toward goals of no consequence.

## The Widow Alone

*for Ilse Hadda*

The journey has at last come to its end.
For the last time I take up his pillow,
fold the sheets, smooth out straight creases. No sound
drifts here from the study, where his mind flew

among the ordinary mysteries
of gods, the cryptic disorders of time.
In our garden, the small red maple grows
without grief, strawberries swell on the stem,

the stones remain still, awaiting a tread
that will not return. Across the Bay's flaked
silver flesh, the city's lights, once bright, brood
through rags of mist. I don't wish to inflict

my loss on anyone; most days, I keep
to myself, file kind letters, wash the car
as if it still mattered, drink from a cup
brittle as bones that grow ever weaker.

The music he loved traces a Baroque
void; verses, philosophies, shape epic
silence. The world's weave is barren fabric,
filled with a voice that can no longer speak.

## A Soldier Writes Home

Continue to commend us,
sneer at those who call war plague,
forgive every hideous
crime that is blessed by a flag.

You know about those bodies:
the army interrogates,
rules get broken, some fool dies.
What haunts me is that boy's guts

writhing like pale snakes in flames,
while the weary Euphrates
lapped at a few ragged palms,
exposing their tender roots.

I won't forget that pagan
child, until I kill again.

## Lachrimæ Pavan

*...shadows that in darkness dwell...*
—John Dowland

You wake to weeping—unaware, at first,
if in some other room a stranger grieves
alone... until the eyes that melt and scald
become your own, while every soul betrayed
is phantomed there, in witness to your pride
and frailty, moaning, *You alone have killed*
*your dreams, with sins you cannot now revise,*
*but must abide within your sleepless breast.*

*

## *Nafs*

As by the shadow of the moon
the solar splendour may appear
eclipsed, so is Spirit hidden
amid the phantoms of our souls.

## Lesson in Mourning

And what of those we never glimpse again:
whom darkness shrouds and silence penetrates
before our wilderness of agony
can be foreseen or consequential rites

prepared? Release them, let sweet flesh subside
and hallow their inevitable grave;
retain the balm that loomed a frail façade.
Far worse to see a living face deprive

you of the gaze it tendered once, the keen
regard that cupped your shape, ensphered with gold
the common bliss of figs unsliced, a broken

loaf, some forgotten tale, a shore recalled.
Succumb, and clutch at worlds erased, sole proof
you ever took a breath bereft of grief.

## Expectant Autumn

Season of winds, accompany my fall:
release the vestiges whose vanished green
did not suffice to freshen or fulfill
the vital task. Come cleanse with your refrain
of bitter mercy every branch, involve
and sweep away the tatters that enslave

these eyes to elegies for fruits I have
not seen, images that never ripened
in my palm, extinguished nectars of that hive
we call the heart. Autumnal angel, expand
your nights, enfold me in your healing wake,
and chasten with your chill the paths I walk.

## Requiem For A Scholar

*In memoriam John K. Walsh*

At last the night has become eternal.
Now his eyes will not glimpse that distant bird
scrawled against the sky's parchment, one carnal
sign in the vast book of the holy bard.

Nor will tongue shape again the sonorous
medieval verse of priests or cavaliers
who sing of swords, grace, victory, sorrows,
disenchantment with the frail world's allures.

He does not linger in the vacant face
but lets wind whisper through his house of bone,
and trusts our harps of memory suffice

to preserve the marvel his life has been
as he moves on, farther than all oceans,
to find out if that fabled light yet shines.

## In Retrospect: Divorce

*...sempre saranno la muta*
*bellezza e il dolore che implora.*
—Lucio Piccolo

To be severed from all you still cherish:
paths hemmed with pine and nasturtiums, adrift
in matins of fog exalting the shore;
scent of roasting *poblanos,* pungent smoke
anointing the night; that motley hammock
gravid with rapturous laughter. To share
no more the zeal that age beguiled, nor craft
a life complete, which grief might never crush.

## Remorse

You have squandered many a fitful night
in lone anguish; yet no voice ever comes
to speak of a path down chambers of flint,
beyond the desolate halls of that maze
your body has become. And the spirit
that filled you with vibrancy has vanished
like a child's whim: amid the smoke and rot
you stagger, an unredeemable shade.
The journey to Rishikesh would not bring
you any nearer to hope; the waters
of Lourdes would smolder in your throat. What sprang
from your sin is immune to sighs or tears,
and your sole pilgrimage lies through a fire
that consumes every sorrow you offer.

## An Elder Nears the End

*...our days travel hand in hand*
*with burning griefs.*
—Rūmī

Horizons fainter... Hopes you might amend
those many faults are but a privilege
of youth elapsed. That gold glint? Tarnished bronze.
And savors pungent once no more amaze.

Yet deathless breath still chisels enigmas
on unvanquished stone, defying ruins.
And earth chants wild psalms of vibrant foliage
whose gardens grace the deserts of the mind.

*

### *Fanā'*

*...until his otherness is drowned in unity.*
– Angelus Silesius

That night on the dune you empty the flask.
A smudge of new moon has orphaned the stars,
denied the sand your shadow. Though you need
to sleep, the vision remains too immense
for dreams, betrayal the only menace:
for you have promised to become the beyond.
Lost at last, you near the source that restores,
inhaling the scent of the One you seek.

## An Oasis

*for Justine Kennedy*

*... whether they are together or apart,*
*he remembers that beauty.*
–Diotima

*The pattern stands so for ever.*
– Kathleen Raine

Do you dare return to sip from the spring
whose waters of remembrance brim with stars
and silence? Undeciphered tracks adorn
its hem of sand, which echoes distances
we neither reach nor dream; yet ancient seas
revive in a gaze where two souls might drown
in one serene communion that destroys
all fear, forgiveness quenching every wrong.

# Canticum Mysterium

*Here... the timeless moment...*
*Never and always.*
–T.S. Eliot

## Canticum Mysterium

A voice cleaves open the hour.
Between the clock's disfigured hands
a rainbow oscillates;
along the brink of anticipation
time apportions its crystals;
light extends its embrace
through the birds' concourse.

Petrified, the earth glistens,
enveloped in modulations of glass,
cold dust on the sleeping roads.
And where, seemingly indolent,
do these bifurcations arrive?
Between what exultant music
and what perilous gesture
are we released to the moment?

We talked as we crossed
the frozen plateau of our memories,
discovering an abandoned path:
artery of weeds returning
to a furtive youth
                                        through which
days unravelled in a skein
of desolate gardens and maternal
admonitions, thoughts in which
the future assumed the shape
of unvanquished cities.
The words we spoke were dust,

a penumbra of desires
                                        exhumed
from childhood's ossuary,
                                              desires
for the pristine clarity
of a distant century
(*in a certain kingdom*
*in a certain land...*),
                                  distressed
virgins, swords of spinning
mercury, Pegasus' ascent
over the turbulent sea:
processions, castles, espionage,
clotted the vernal brain.

Yet how can we lament the lost
fragrance of those years?
No rage assailed the tender eyes,
our simple games bereft of perfidy,
kisses rendered under a willow
sheltering lips from fervor;
but innocence
                          was a siege
committed to devouring
                                              the pulse
of a mystery we could not yet imagine:
secluded behind eyes untouched
by the winding world,
how could we know that this ceremony
of being and becoming
is no relentless advance,
but a tremulous winging
toward the penultimate
                                             absence
that satiates the absolute?

Only

today
can I discern
what once these same eyes
saw but could not perceive.
Now,
with the past more visible
than that tenuous present
which could not contain itself
and ruptured into history,
past
uprooted from insomnias and dazes,
diffused across the table
like a gnarled parable:
in knots, spirals,
the voluptuous agonies revive,
exist again, as though time
had dilated and drawn the memories
into a vortex culminating
here,
streaming
into the room inhabited
by the man those ancient
seconds devised from a raw,
amorphous boy.

As a child,
exiled
to the dark velocity of dreams,
there was a window
I could never open,
suspended
in the tangled geometry
of that house which was not
a place but a palpable
event
where, little by little,
silhouetted gestures stained

the immaculate walls
and faces sprang up
from the vitrified
                    silence
of a mirror in an empty room.

Unendurable nights,
                    water issuing
from a remote piano,
                    names
traced in that water,
                    winds
rummaging the dark ivy
                    for a voice.

In the casement,
                    a spider's tomb:
reticular cacophany,
filamental threnody
for a shadowed life
                    that voyaged
the night's hours
                    knitting
air to space.

*"There's no escape,"*
I heard my father whisper
into his glass of bourbon.

I learned not to seek answers:
in my pockets I collected questions,
savored, tended them,
                    as others
harbored coins or cigarettes.
Contemplation was a flight
from the barren nausea
of classrooms and cluttered

corridors where loneliness
festered at the root
of garrulous tongues;
                                        to wander
through the pages
                                  of Parmenides
was more a yearning than
a search;
                to shape
sinuous lips into the serene
convulsion
                    of a butterfly
                                            (in order
to pronounce
                        those chimerical
names:
              Avalokiteshvara,
                                              Zoroaster)
was to perceive an inscription
in the dim revolving of the blood:
The impossible
                            exists
because we conceive it:

miraculous time and its conventicles,
eternity and its rivers,
                                        shadow
poised in the moon's core,
sable firmament aspersed with gleamings.

Spirit,
            sun,
                    clay,
                              grass,
                                        oats,
                                                  fish
                                                        and oxen

invented us;
we composed
the gods and their dreams:
woman,
man,
horse,
lizard,
wheat,
soil,
star.

There is no beginning.
The dreamer is the reflection
of his dream,
fever that burst forth
from the weary eye in sleep
to summon the inventory
of imagination,
unite its threads
with a lutanist's grace.

Pliny saw a centaur preserved in honey.
Not an illusion:
the flesh of a man
made one body with that of a horse,
dense mane emerging from a human spine.

Centaurs, sphinxes, simurghs,
chimerae
cease to exist
only when we no longer dream them.

In the south I watched a man
open a stone with his fingers
and raise it to his face:
when the hand descended
milk

still glistened on his lips.

Once I witnessed a woman
draw from her thighs
a living being.
                    With a cry
of annunciation,
                        that child
transfigured the world.

Every birth is unique.

All deaths
are but a single dying,
alchemy that gnaws, devours,
blights and blinds,
transmutes, revives,
                            and becomes
the same.
              That very child
who dreams again those memories
lost among wrinkles,
                             in the chasm
of assembled hours,
                            forsaken
in the attrition of a ceaseless
                                       wheel,
wheel of the return,
wheel of the death cart
where all the corpses of the planet
are heaped.

We are born in solitude.
                                  Death
sweeps us into the indiscriminate
windrows of a common grave:
Eucharist of silent tongues and maggots,

threshold that mediates
between
eternity and oblivion.

Both are here,
present
in this room:
the unforgettable
and the forsaken,
river
and abyss,
lashed
and balanced
by the dream.
Not of innocence:
the sentient dream
of existence,
sharp dream with open eyes
that unleashes the weight of the centuries
in a lucid instant
which lasts forever.

In the same room
death and being
confront each other.
Mask and mirror,
they seek each other out,
fabricating chaos and mortality
among pencils and discarded clothing,
sustaining a duel in which neither
prevails.

In the same room,
a man
and a woman,
exchanging faces,
naked.

Flesh:
water and silk.

We have arrived
in the moment.
We are here,
converging
between death and its mask,
being and its mirror.
Our bodies
dream each other.
Between your thighs you enfold
both petal and fruit;
in grazing your flesh
my lips
drift
across the face of the world,
and sparrows rise
from your gestures.
You offer your breath to me:
with my hands,
I sustain you,
unlock your body to the winds.

In your eyes,
mystery
beyond innocence.
You are a rage,
fury
consumed with stillness:
tranquility ardently wrought.

We open the door:
through that space
the room dissolves
into twilight without limits.

Against the horizon,
                                        branches poise,
solemn nets draped over a sphere.
Bark rasps against bark:
through the limbs
                                    a door
opening on the stars.
                                        The trees
are dreaming: green spires,
flowers of fire,
                            sky
brimmed with pollen.

In the garden where we wait,
                                                    it rains;
myriad voices
                            shatter on tiles,
transparent worlds falling,
                                                breathing,
yielding their shape,
                                        returning
to the unspeaking mouth
of the eloquent earth.

We come to understand,
                                            here
among shadows where our blood
is turning with that same
diluvial persistence:
the earth, too, has its voices.

Darkness
                sings.

<u>Notes</u>: *The Shadow of Gabriel's Wing*

<u>Epigraphs</u>:

Sachiko Murata, "The Angels." In *Islamic Spirituality: Foundations*, ed. Seyyed Hossein Nasr (New York: Crossroads, 1987), 229-30.

Anna Akhmatova, "I ask you to pray for my poor... living soul..." (Zh. 85), in *The Complete Poems of Anna Akhmatova*, trans. Judith Hemschemeyer. Expanded ed. (Boston: Zephyr, 1997), 150-1.

**I. Mirabilium**

<u>Epigraph</u>: "Meantime let wonder seem familiar..."
*Much Ado About Nothing* (5.4.69) {Friar Francis}.

*

SOSPIRI –

<u>Epigraphs</u>:

Nicola Benedetti: *In Focus* lecture supplementing her performance of Szymanowski's Violin Concerto #1 (Royal Scottish National Orchestra, 11 Mar., 2021). Yet her words obviously apply to her exquisite recording of Elgar's *Sospiri*, and her utterance reaches far beyond: to that state of consciousness where awe and wonder, humility and fragility are the only apt response to the metaphysical reality evoked in this sonnet: our immersion the Beautiful and the Sublime, our dignity and evanescence: the infinitesimal conjoined with the Infinite.

A.W. Schlegel (1767-1845) contrasted "the poetry of the Ancients," characterized by "possession" (*Besitzes*), with Romantic poetry, whose essence is longing (*Sehnsucht*). The quote (*die Poesie der Alten war die des Besitzes, die unsrige ist die der Sehnsucht...*) is from Lilian R. Furst, *European Romanticism: Self-Definition* (London: Methuen, 1980), pp. 34, 36.

Several strands inspired this sonnet: Sir Edward Elgar's *Sospiri* (Op. 70) was first performed in August, 1914, twelve days after Germany declared war on France. Originally written for string orchestra, harp and chamber organ, the poignancy of the piece is intensified in the later transcription for piano and violin, whose "sighs" embody ineffable yearning and frailty.

The final thread, and catalyst of the poem, was the gift of Justine Kennedy's graced response to contemplating images mapping Laniakea, the supercluster in which the entire Milky Way is but a pinhead. The mysteries of Soul, Communion, Nature, Cosmos: concentric spheres provoking awe, reverence, yearning, sighs that chime with Shakespeare's words: "...'tis wonder that enwraps me thus..." {*Twelfth Night* (4.3.1)}.

*

ANANTA RAGA -

*Ananta:* endless, eternal. Also the name of the world-serpent on which Vishnu rests.
*Rāgā:* neither melody nor mode, a Rāgā is rather a melodic structure that rises or falls, a constellation of notes having specific ratios to their tonic. It is thus the configuration upon which the sitar player improvises; comprising both pattern and passion, each Rāgā corresponds to a specific color and mood, a time of day, and a season of the year.

Abhinavagupta (950-1020 AD): leading exponent of Kashmir Śaivism, referred to by his disciples as Mahamaheśvara, "great devotee of Śivā." The core of his philosophy, *Pratyabhijñā* ("recognition"), is that liberation consists in realizing that the Lord's real presence resides in all things: the soul, *ātman*, is thus an image or mirror of the divine. The epigraph is from his *Tantrāloka*, I.192.

*Alāp*: The musical invocation or unveiling of the Rāgā's form. Ravi Shankar has referred to it as disclosing "the face of the Rāgā," and as an "unfolding, like describing a beautiful body."

Five syllables: the "five syllable mantra" is *Śivāya namah*, "Hail to Śivā." Its repetition is held to lead to the direct awareness of the unity of opposites.

Lotus throne: *padmāsana*, indicating spiritual purity, divinity. In yoga, the "lotus pose."

*Purusha* and *prakriti*: respectively, spirit and nature, day and night, essence and form, the male and female principles.

*Tāla*: the rhythmic structure of Indian music, expressed by the tablā or hand drums.

*Rasavant*: A work of art possessing *Rasa*: beauty, essence, flavor, also implying color and mood, and often identified with the divine. *Rasa* is the essential element in traditional Indian poetry, not meter or rhyme. The lover or connoisseur of art is *rasika*. See Ananda K. Coomaraswamy, *The Dance of Shiva*.

Chidambaram: As Natarāja, Lord of the Dance, Śivā danced in Chidambaram or Tillai, the Golden Hall at the center of the universe, which is the human heart. He is represented with his four hands moving, one holding the drum whose rhythm creates the cosmos, another the flame that destroys: his dance burns away darkness, ignorance and evil, and releases the seeker from the fetters of illusion.

Vīrabhadra: An avatar of Śivā as both protector of sages and fierce warrior who battles against demons. In this form, Śivā dances on the ghats among incinerated corpses, goblins and ghosts, the dance of destruction, complement and counterpoint to Natarāja's cosmic dance. One of Vīrabhadra's several temples is located in Bangalore.

Ardhanārīshvara: The form of God that is female on the left, male on the right, according to Śaiva Siddhānta tradition. Literally, the Lord (*Iśvara*) that is half (*ardha*) woman (*nāri*): God and his grace are indivisible.

*Garbha*: womb. *Garbha grha* refers to the innermost sanctuary of a temple.

*Anugraha*: divine grace, favor.

Kalidasa: (ca. 350-420) considered the greatest poet of classical Sanskrit, he composed both epic poems and dramas incorporating music and dance. According to legend, he received his gift from the goddess Kali, the mother-aspect of Śiva.

*

THE OMNIVOYANT GAZE -

Epigraph: Nicholas of Cusa's *On the Vision of God*, 6.21.

In 1453, Nicholas, Bishop of Brixen-Bresssanone (Tyrol), sent his treatise *De visione Dei sive De icona* [*On the Vision of God, or On the Icon*] to the monks at Tegernsee (Bavaria). The treatise—a masterpiece of mystical contemplation emphasizing the unity of Love and Knowledge on the path to union with God—was accompanied by an Icon of the Divine Face, which from any angle in a room, seemed to gaze solely at each observer, thus symbolizing the transcendence of space and time, and embracing all of creation. Nicholas suggests the

convergence of our seeing and being seen by God, wherein we ourselves become symbols of the Divine.
(v. 3): The icon was lost long ago; we can only infer that it embodied Christ as the Face of all faces.
(v. 7): The Phoenix, since it built a nest of spices upon which it immolated itself before being reborn from its ashes, was a symbol of Christ from the earliest Christian centuries and beyond; before that it appeared in Chinese art and myth as *feng huang*, (male and female, transcending opposites), associated with birth and conception; and famously in Egypt, where it was associated with the resurrection of Osiris. Greek and Roman writers, from Herodotus to Pliny the Elder, frequently mentioned the Phoenix. {cf. Louis Charbonneau-Lassay, *The Bestiary of Christ*. 1941, trans. D.M. Dooling (New York: Parabola Books, 1991), pp. 441-52.}
(v. 8): Throughout the Gospel of John, a pervasive thread recurs: blindness as a spiritual state, transcended by visionary seeing and knowing (*gnosis*, forms of which occur over 200 times in the New Testament) {see, e.g., John 1:10, 7:26, 8:55, 10:38, 12:16; and esp. John 14:17, 14:20, 16:3, 17:3; and the Letter, 1 John 2:13-14, 3:1, 4:6-8, 4:16, 5:20}.
*

LEGIBLE -
Epigraphs:
St. Bonaventure, *The Soul's Journey into God*, 2.11; Adi Śankara, *Ātma-bodha*, 16.
*

ANGEL OF THE SPANDREL -
In the Cologne Cathedral Choir, angels are depicted in the arcade spandrels, elevated above the apostles, inviting us to attune ourselves to the presence of celestial music, lest "The man that hath no music in himself" fail to "change his nature." {*Merchant of Venice* 5.1.80-1.}
*

*SFUMATO: ARS PINGENDI* -
The sonnet was inspired by Leonardo da Vinci's conception and practice of *sfumatura*, the shading of colours subtly blended "without lines or borders, in the manner of smoke."
*

MONASTERY –
San Antolín de Bedón is a thirteenth-century Benedictine monastery near Naves, on the coast of Asturias, encircled by meadows through which the Bedón River disembogues into the Cantabrian Sea. José Luis Puerto's poems, some of which I have been fortunate to translate, are particularly sensitive to the haunting presence of the past inscribed in both nature and culture.
*

BECAUSE THEY HAVE FORSAKEN –
To my knowledge, no one has previously granted the adulteress a voice.
*

*DE NATURA SONORIS* –
Jorge Martínez García (b. 1963) is a renowned Chilean neo-Baroque painter. The sonnet was written only days before discovering his painting of the same name; the affinity I felt for his radiant work provoked the dedication.

A selection of his works can be viewed at http://www.jorgemartinezgarcia.com/
*

COMMUNION –
The dedicatee is Rev. Adrian Pearce, of St. Ambrose, Bournemouth.
*

CARTOGRAPHY –
After many years of admiring his work, especially his legendary portrayal of Sir Thomas More, I met the great actor Paul Scofield (1922-2008)—by chance or providence—on a train from Calais to Paris. Our friendship, correspondence and phone conversations spanned some fifteen years. Beyond death he remains the single most gracious person I have ever met. Dame Helen Mirren put it aptly: "He aspires to the soul rather than the character. He has no sense of personal ambition."
*

*WINTERREISE* –
The title echoes Schubert's great song cycle (*Winter Journey*, Op. 89, 1827-8), from poems by Wilhelm Müller. The cycle's wistful lyricism enchanted Sir Benjamin Britten, who returned to it again and again, only to find that "each time, the mystery remains."

The internal quote from my son Sebastian Balthazar reproduces his exact words at age five, as a crepuscular blizzard descended to envelop the highway, reducing visibility to mere inches, entirely obscuring the road ahead: *der Weg gehüllt in Schnee...*
*

ELIXIR –
An acrostic variant of a sonnet; the first letters of its fifteen verses spell out my daughter's first and middle name.

**II. Legendarium**

Epigraph: *..là où commence / Le pays qui ne sait que l'éternel...* (...there, where begins / ...The country that knows only eternity...)Yves Bonnefoy, "Le puis, les ronces," *In the Shadow's Light* [*Ce qui fut sans lumière*] (Chicago: U of Chicago P, 1991), p. 40.

That country, to my mind, is the realm of imagination, myth, legend, dream: visions that time does not efface.
*

A RING OF ANCIENT STONES -
Pentre Ifan in Pembrokeshire is today a dolmen comprising seven megaliths, the skeletal remains of a Neolithic burial chamber at least 5,000 years old, near the Preseli Hills, whose volcanic and igneous "bluestones" were also used in the construction of Stonehenge.
*

UNHOLY TERRITORY -
Bathos: here the Titans made their last, fatal stand against the Olympian gods. Hephaestus and Hecate participated in the defeat. See Robert Graves, *Greek Myths*, Vol. 1, ch. 35.
*

XENOPHANES -
The $6^{th}$-century BC philosopher-poet of Colophon is renowned not for atheism, as sometimes supposed, but for repudiating the tendency to anthropomorphize the gods, and thereby allow them to commit immoral acts.

Two of his extant fragments are of particular note:

*But if horses or oxen or lions had hands or could draw with their hands and accomplish such works as men, horses would draw the figures of the gods as similar to horses, and the oxen as similar to oxen, and they would make the bodies of the sort which each of them had* (frag. 15); and *Homer and Hesiod have attributed to the gods all sorts of things which are matters of reproach and censure among men: theft, adultery and mutual deceit* (frag. 11).

Plato, on similar grounds, would object to literalizing the myths, while proffering his own myths in their stead, such as the Myth of Metals and the Myth of Er (cf. *Republic*, Bk. III; Bk. X).

*

LETTER FROM TARSUS -

Athenodorus of Tarsus (Cananites) (c. 74 BC-7 AD) was born near Tarsus, became the teacher of Cesar Augustus, and was known to Pliny the Younger.

Like the speaker in the poem, many Romans regarded Tarsus as an insignificant but rather pretentious backwater. It was nonetheless a place where Jewish and Greco-Roman culture mingled.

Saul of Tarsus, from a family of Jewish tentmakers, would become St. Paul.

*

ENCOUNTER WITH ASTERION -

Epigraph: Jorge Luis Borges, "House of Asterion," in *Borges: A Reader*. Ed. Emir Rodríguez Monegal and Alastair Reid (New York: Dutton, 1981, p. 196).

Asterion ("starry one") is the proper name of the Minotaur of Cnossos on Crete. He was the child of Queen Pasiphaë and the "bull from the sea" sent by Poseidon in answer to King Minos' prayer, confirming that his sovereignty was divinely bestowed. Though promising to sacrifice the sacred bull, Minos substituted another; as a result Poseidon contrived that Pasiphaë should conceive a lust for the bull. Thanks to the artifice of Daedalus, the bull mated with the queen, whose issue was Asterion. (Pseudo-Apollodorus, *Bibliotheca* 3. 8-11). The monster was confined in "the coiled habitation of the crooked labyrinth" (Callimachus, Hymn 4 to Delos, 311 ff [trans. Mair]), which was also devised by Daedalus (Pseudo-Apollodorus, *Bibliotheca* 3. 213). Falsely believing that the Athenians were responsible for the death of his son Androgeos, Minos demanded retributive sacrifices to the Minotaur of either seven youths and maidens every nine years. (Pausanias, *Description of Greece* 1.27.10). Ariadne, daughter of Minos, helped Theseus to navigate the labyrinth (Diodorus Siculus, *Library of History* 4.61.4).

Asterion was also the name of a god, and of the river in Argos that bears his name, as well as a plant that grew on its banks, from whose leaves garlands were woven for Hera (Pausanias 2.17.1-2).

*

PHIDIAS IN OLYMPIA -

Phidias, or Pheidias (c. 480-430 BC), the most eminent sculptor in Ancient Greece, was commissioned to fashion the chryselephantine (gold and ivory) statue that would be housed in the Temple of Zeus at Olympia, in the Elis district (Western Peloponnese); the statue took twelve years to complete and was deemed one of the Seven Wonders of the Ancient World. Some six centuries later, the temple and statue are painstakingly detailed in Pausanias' *Description of Greece* (Bk. 5.10-11). The Eleans were custodians of the Olympic games, over which the statue of Zeus would preside until 393 AD, when the games were abolished by the Emperor Flavius Honorius, son of Theodosius I.

(v. 9): Phidias fashioned several sculptures of Athena, including the bronze Promachos (c. 460 BC) and the chryselephantine Parthenos (c. 447-438 BC), both on the Acropolis in Athens.
(vv. 25-6): Phidias' wealth was legendary (cf. Plato, *Meno* 91d), and shortly after the dedication of the Parthenos, he was accused by Menon, one of his workmen, of embezzling gold intended for the statue; he was further accused of impiety (Plutarch, *Life of Pericles*, 31). Plutarch erroneously claims that Phidias died in prison—quite impossible, given that his Olympian Zeus was completed several years later. Rather, after the trial, he is thought to have fled to Elis (Philochorus, Fragment 121).
(vv. 34-5): The sculptor's conspicuous friendship with Pericles provoked attacks on Phidias and others by the statesman's enemies. (Plutarch 13.9; 31.4).
(vv. 38-41): Pericles had studied philosophy with Zeno and with Anaxagoras, who famously argued that the order of the world resulted from intelligence, rather than either chance or necessity. Becoming notorious for his skill at sophistry, Pericles neglected Anaxagoras, who nearly died of starvation, and his role as "champion of the people" is dubious, even in Thucydides: a cunning disguise for demagoguery in the service of militarism and imperialism—indeed symbolizing "the tragedy of Athens and his age": embodying the city's illusions of "Athenian imperial greatness" in his own "delusions of power" [Edith Foster, *Thucydides, Pericles, and Periclean Imperialism* (Cambridge UP, 2010), p. 121, 181, 188].
(v. 49-50): The Altis was the sacred precinct of Zeus at Olympia, containing not only temples and statues, but the most sacred grove of plane trees (Old World sycamore), as well as olive, poplar, oak and pine.
Two rivers: the Kladeos and Alpheios, whose streams merge near the sanctuary. (Pausanias 5.10.6; 5.15.6).
(v. 57): *Lord of Time* is one of Zeus' epithets: cf. Aeschylus, *The Suppliants*, Chorus Strophe 4, Morshead trans.
(vv. 101-2): Various epithets of Zeus: Meilichíos, an ancient chthonic deity absorbed by Zeus: he who must be propitiated, yet is gracious, mild, and purifies after the shedding of kindred blood (cf. Pausanias 2.20.1-2); his cult in Athens was celebrated in the Diasia festival.

Zeus Horkios, protector of the sanctity of oaths.

Zeus Xenios, protector of hospitality, of guests and strangers.

(vv. 105-9): Phidias' workshop in Elis, west of the Temple of Zeus, was excavated in 1958 by a team of German archeologists led by Emil Kunze, amid the ruins of a Christian basilica destroyed by earthquake in 551 AD. The remains included terracotta moulds, tools, and scraps of ivory. The sole personal item discovered was a small black wine cup bearing the inscription: "I am of Pheidias" (Φειδίου εἰμί).

The exact circumstances of the statue's destruction is uncertain: probably stripped of its gold under Constantine (c. 330 AD) to adorn Constantinople, it may have reached the city when statues were removed from temples (c. 408). It was later housed in the palace of Lausos, the eunuch and grand chamberlain to Theodosius II (402-50); Lausos' menagerie of statues numbered at least thirteen, including Zeus, Hera, Athena, Aphrodite, unicorns and centaurs, and was perhaps intended to suggest the humiliation of pagan idols. After Lausus' death (c. 440?), Phidias' masterpiece probably perished in the fire of 475, which consumed the palace, rather than the fire of 532, when half the city burned during the Nika revolt. {cf. Sarah Guberti Bassett, "'Excellent Offerings': The Lausos Collection in Constantinople." *The Art Bulletin* 82.1 (2000): 6-25.}

*

LEOPARDI -

Epigraph: *...nascere al pianto...* (...born to weep...) from "Inno ai Patriarchi o de' principii del genere umano" (v. 7).

Giacomo Leopardi was both a classical philologist and the most eminent and philosophical poet in 19th-century Italy, at once Romantic and anti-Romantic, renowned for the "brilliant bleakness" of his "magnificently desolate poems", in the words of Adam Kirsch. Though often labeled simply "pessimistic", his *Canti* and other works fearlessly address the human condition as a tragic diapason that embraces beauty and despair, serenity and misery, joy and disillusion. Despite a pervasive materialism and nihilism, his work offers a salutary antidote to the ills of modernity, whose facile optimism and fatuous denialism masquerade as hope, fostering and enabling our current Age of Delusions and Distractions.

*

THE SCORPION -

Epigraphs: Nikos Karouzos, "Continuing City", in *Modern European Poetry*, ed. Willis Barnstone, et al. (New York: Bantam, 1966), 264.
Lord Byron, *The Giaour* (v. 430).

Amid the ancient lore of scorpions we find the notion that a scorpion will sting itself to death rather than be consumed by fire {Shelley: "And we are left, as scorpions ringed with fire / What should we do but sting ourselves to death?" (*Cenci* II.ii, 70-1)}.

When Orion vowed to kill all the beasts, Gaia sent the Scorpion to slay him; the bravery of both destined them as constellations. Yet when Scorpio rises in the East, Orion sets, "as a lesson to men not to be too self-confident." (Pseudo-Hyginus, *Astronomica* 2. 26. cf.: Aratus, *Phaenomena* 634 ff.; Ovid, *Fasti* 5. 493 ff.)

In Egyptian myth, following Seth's murder of Osiris, seven scorpions were sent by Thoth to protect Isis and Horus, as they sought refuge from the fratricide. The scorpion appeared on the headdress of the goddess Selket (Serqet or Serket), who came to be regarded as an aspect of Isis. She both heals from the scorpion's or serpent's poison, and harms the unrighteous: her name may be translated as "She Who Tightens Throats," since the venom's victim is left breathless; or as "She Who Lets Throats Breathe," since she gave breath to the dead, that they might be reborn in the afterlife. Selket was also said to accompany Ra in his nightly journey through the underworld, protecting him against the evil serpent-demon Apep.

A solar parallel is found in the *Epic of Gilgamesh* (Tablet IX), where scorpion-men guard the mountain threshold of the netherworld, opening the doors for Shamash the sun god when he emerges each day, and shutting them behind him when he returns to the underworld at night.

One of the scorpion-men warns Gilgamesh that "no one goes beyond..." Undaunted by the threat of twelve leagues of darkness, Gilgamesh vows to go on, "gasping after breath." The same phrase is used for Enkidu and Humbaba, as well, suggesting the mortality and finitude that the hero seeks to overcome.

After traveling the "hidden road of the sunrise," he reaches the radiant garden of the gods, with its foliage of lapis lazuli, carnelian and rubies. He famously fails, however, to gain the immortality for which he yearns.

Only after writing the poem did I discover that my scorpion, with his Stoic poise and pride, presents a counterpoint to the tortured soul in Byron's *Giaour* (1813), vv. 422-38:

> *The mind that broods o'er guilty woes,*
> *Is like the scorpion girt by fire;*
> *In circle narrowing as it glows,*
> *The flames around their captive close,*
> *Till inly searched by thousand throes,*
> *And maddening in her ire,*
> *One sad and sole relief she knows,*
> *The sting she nourished for her foes,*
> *Whose venom never yet was vain,*
> *Gives but one pang, and cures all pain,*
> *So do the dark in soul expire,*
> *Or live like scorpion girt by fire;*
> *So writhes the mind remorse hath riven,*
> *Unfit for earth, undoomed for heaven,*
> *Darkness above, despair beneath,*
> *Around it flame, within it death!*

*

THE COUNT -

Epigraph: Baudelaire, "Le Vampire".

My sonnet elaborates upon the common idea of Dracula as an anguished, tragic figure, adding the notion that he yearns to be subject to the vagaries of ordinary mortals.

*

A NOTEBOOK OF 1920 -

Epigraph: Rainer Maria Rilke purchased a notebook, following his return to Paris in 1920, inscribing the first page with the phrase *Ici commence l'indecible*: "Here begins the unsayable". The remaining leaves of the notebook are entirely blank {cf. Wolfgang Leppmann. *Rilke: A Life*, trans. Russell M. Stockman (New York: Fromm, 1984)}.

*

TABOR -

(for the Feast of the Transfiguration)

I. *Anabasis*

Ancient Greeks and Romans used messengers (*anabasii*) to bring messages and commands long distances. The apostles are messengers... The Transfiguration on Tabor is initiatic: Peter, James and John are the first called to be transformed. They stand prepared to be imbued with divine participation with Christ: *theosis*: God became man that man might become God (St. Irenaeus, St. Athanasius). Contrast to Arrian's *Anabasis Alexandri*, the account of Alexander's military conquests, rife with brutality, corruption and delusion.

(v. 5): *phosphor* –Venus; "the morning star which never sets" becomes Christ as bearer of light (Lucifer) in the words of the *Exsultet for Easter* sung during the Easter Vigil ("*Flammas eius lucifer matutinus inveniat: ille, inquam, lucifer,qui nescit occasum, Christus Filius tuus...*") Greek *Phosphoros* "morning star," literally "torchbearer," from *phos*, "light," contraction of *phaos* "light, daylight"+ *phoros* "bearer," from *pherein* "to carry." Venus, the Morning Star, is also a type of the Virgin, *theotokos*, the bearer of God. Thus phosphor invokes both Mary and Christ: she who bears the light, and He who bears Divinity.

The element phosphorus was not recorded until 17th c. by Brand, who wrote to Leibniz about it; though it may have been known to 12th c. Arabic alchemists. Brand derived phosphorus from urine, an apt symbol of the transformation of the soul from noxious sin to *theosis*: restoration of the Divine image and likeness.

II. *Katabasis* – descent, going down, including a descent into Hell or the Underworld.
cf. The descent of Orpheus (*Metamorphoses* X), Odysseus (*Odyssey* XI) and Aeneas (*Aeneid* VI). The Apostles' descent of the mountain into the quotidian world is a figure of Christ's descent into Hell to free souls from death and distance from God.
(v. 15): *taint* – not only tinge of colour or dye, in contrast to the pure white of the Transfiguration, but of course the sense of stain, blemish, disgrace, cause of corruption or decay. Sins are but signs: for the nature of our particular sins adumbrate the virtues that summon us: lust, for example, is potentially charity; *acedia* or sloth is potentially serenity, surrender, the gift of contemplation.
*tincture* – also "dye", but also a quality imparted – in Alchemy, a spiritual principle or substance or quintessence whose virtues may be infused into physical things. A tincture is thought to possess the power to extract the essential virtues of any herb. Paracelsus refers to the Red Lion, a tincture he calls "the element of fire which stands above the water, the air, and the earth."

In Christian alchemy, whose symbolism appears in many of the greatest mystics, such as St. Teresa of Avila, it is the soul that is transformed from lead to gold, deriving from Job: "But he knoweth the way that I take: when he hath tried me [in the crucible], I shall come forth as gold" (23:10). The tincture symbolises Christ himself, often referred to as the true Philosopher's Stone, whilst the soul of gold symbolises "the regaining of the original nobility of human nature." {Titus Burckhardt, *Alchemy: Science of the Cosmos, Science of the Soul*, trans. William Stoddart (Baltimore: Penguin, 1971), 26.}
*

THE VACANT CROSS -
The sonnet addresses the theological problem of presenting the empty cross in churches, as if to efface the suffering that life entails in favour of a "happy ending", which contributes to the failure of compassion in the face of the human sacrifice inflicted upon all children of God, regardless of creed, under the idolatrous names of "progress", "national defense", "economic necessity" and the narcissism of religious exclusivism.
*

CARVED VIRGIN -
A humble, exquisitely carved modern Virgin in St. Stephan's, Mainz—her robe encompassing faces peering up in hope—is unduly neglected in light of the attention paid to Marc Chagall's renowned stained glass windows.

**III. Eros / Algos**

Epigraph: Kathleen Raine, "*As a Hurt Child...*" in *Collected Poems*, Washington, D.C.: Counterpoint, 2001), p. 259.

*Eros* is not limited to the erotic aspects of sensual passion, but rather the cosmic principle of love, attraction and union, which Homer and later Empedocles saw as operating in conjunction and tension with Eris, the principle of discord and strife, personified as the sister of Ares. Eros entails the convergence of souls. In the *Symposium*, Plato presents Eros as neither wholly divine nor solely human, a spirit whose sensual aspect is but a prelude to the yearning for transcendental Beauty (210a-212a). This is reflected in Christian Eros: experience of the other not as an object of lustful desire, but an image of sacred beauty and goodness, and union as sacramental {cf. Philip Sherrard, *Christianity and Eros: Essays on the Theme of Sexual Love* (Limni, Greece: Denise Harvey, 2002)}.

*Algos* is pain, whence derive our words neuralgia and nostalgia... Hesiod uses the plural form *Algea* to designate the three daughters of Eris, personifications of anguish, grief and sorrow (*Theogony* 227).

*

APOTHEOSIS OF EARTHLY LOVE -

The sonnet is addressed to Orpheus, whose love for Eurydice is not rooted in mere passion, but summoned in response to the Divine Feminine. Plato, however, suggests that the poet's failure and fate—being punished by the gods at the hands of women who stoned and ripped him apart—resulted from weakness, contrasting him with Alcestis, who was willing to remain in Hades in exchange for her husband's life (*Symposium* 79d-e).

*

NUPTIALS -

Epigraph: The exact source of Ibn 'Arabi's quote has been lost to me, but the idea that Nature is "a mirror where God sees his form" is found not only in the *Meccan Revelations* (*Al-Futuhat al-Makkiyah*), but throughout Sufi tradition: "Everything in the cosmos manifests the names and attributes of God..." Rumi famously asserts: "The world is like a mirror displaying Love's perfection", just as the human being as microcosm is both a mirror of all things and a manifestation of the divine attributes {cf. William C. Chittick, *The Sufi Path of Love: The Spiritual Teachings of Rumi* (Albany: SUNY, 1983), 197, 62, 65.}

My epithalamium alludes to Ibn 'Arabi's vision that not only is marriage sacred, but that "witnessing God in the female form is the most perfect mode of witnessing", since in Woman Man beholds "both yang and yin... both majesty and beauty (*jalal* & *jamal*), distance and nearness, activity and receptivity {cf. Sachiko Murata, *The Tao of Islam: A Sourcebook on Gender Relationships in Islamic Thought* (Albany: SUNY, 1992), 37-9, 192.}

*

ECSTASY -

As John O'Donohue observed: "...the mystery of making love... is not just two bodies... but rather two worlds; they circle each other and flow into each other." {*Anam Cara: A Book of Celtic Wisdom* (New York: Harper Perennial, 1998), pp. 40-1.}

*

CLEFT AND CLASP -

Epigraph: Andrew Marvell, "The Garden" (vv. 61-4).

My sonnet is a riposte to Marvell (1621-78), whose eloquent verses praise Nature and contemplation, yet idealize egoic solitude, seeing the lavish garden he admires as an echo of paradise only insofar as it pleases the private self. His rejection of the vanity of ambition in public life (vv. 1-4) is thus not countered but merely displaced by the vanity of autonomy. The true paradisaic state is harmony, conjunction, communion, the union of opposites: Cusanus' *coincidentia oppositorum*, Taoism's *yin/yang*. In this light, the wit of Marvell's poem is not simply misogynistic or misanthropic, but inclines toward narcissism, its metaphysical premises being fallacious as well as blasphemous.

Contrary to common ahistorical assumptions, Eve was by no means always held to blame for the Fall: other interpretations blamed both Adam and Eve, while many, such as that of St. Bernard, condemned Adam for his cowardice; and the *Theologia Germanica* presents the Fall as resulting from the "I, me, mine": the idolatry of the individual will and its specious aseity, seduced by the Serpent's delusive promise: "You shall be as gods."

*

CUNNILINGUS -

Epigraph: Octavio Paz, "Eje" ("Axis"), in *A Draft of Shadows*, trans. Eliot Weinberger (New York: New Directions, 1979), p. 22.

Form embodies content: the two sestets are mirrored quatrains ending in couplets, manifesting the complementarity of male and female and their coalescence: the interpenetration of souls, as figured in the slant-rhyme scheme: a/b/c/d/e/e/d/c/b/a/f/f/.

*

AN OLD GREEK NUN RECALLS HER YOUTH -

The second stanza refers to a long-established Greek tradition on the eve of the midsummer Feast of St. John the Baptist (23 June; O.S. Calendar 11 June).

*

BEFORE THE SUMMER -

Epigraph: Anne Morrow Lindbergh, *Gift from the Sea*. 1955 (New York: Pantheon, 1975), p. 76.

**IV. Lachrymae Rerum**

Epigraph: Virgil, *Aeneid*, Book 1.461. The literal translation is "These are the tears of things, and our mortality touches the mind/heart."Seamus Heaney renders it as "There are tears at the heart of things."

These are the words of Aeneas as he stands in the temple of Juno in Carthage, beholding a mural that depicts the battle of Troy, which Aeneas has survived amidst devastating loss and sorrow.

All glory is fleeting; all that is lovely, noble and precious ultimately perishes. The tragic evanescence, fragility and caducity of life has for centuries been a major theme of Western poetry—not least of all in the Metaphysical Poets of the 17th century, such as John Donne—as well as in music, most notably John Dowland's *Lachrimæ*, and in the magnificent still life *Vanitas* paintings of the Baroque (exemplified in Pieter Claesz and Balthasar van der Ast) depicting lustrous fruit in perfect ripeness, flowers, culinary delicacies, exquisite lutes and viols, books and necklaces—in counterpoint with the ominous presence of an overturned goblet, an empty shell, a shriveling grape, a bruised petal, perhaps a fly, a watch, often a skull: *Memento mori*.

The theme has its analogue in the Japanese *mono no aware*—the "pathos of things" that honours the wistful, poignant awareness of life's ineluctable sorrow.

The implication is not of suffering as merely subjective and private, but rather that the world laments with us—for until the atomistic, "corpuscular philosophy" that conceived of Nature as merely dead bits of matter, the entire cosmos was seen as ensouled: animated and even encompassed by Intelligence, Spirit, abrim with spirits and angels. The maturity to face and embrace melancholy, to invite the heart to melt, is among the many virtues that the modern obsession with self-satisfaction has discarded at our peril.

In his contribution to the "Before I Die" project, James A. Reeves captured beautifully the significance of the idea: "*Lacrimae rerum* can become an organizing principle, reminding us that we are surrounded by compassion while we mourn."
https://beforeidieproject.com/crying/

UNDISCLOSED -
Epigraph:
Victor Hugo: "*La mélancolie est un crépuscule. La souffrance s'y fond dans une sombre joie. La mélancolie, c'est le bonheur d'être triste.*" ("Melancholy is a twilight. Suffering melts into it in sombre joy. Melancholy is the happiness of being sad." {*The Toilers of the Sea*, trans. Isabel F. Hapgood, Vol. 2, 3.1.1: "The Bell of the Port" (New York: Thomas Y. Crowell, 1888), p. 196}.

A more readily available edition is Victor Hugo, *The Toilers of the Sea*, trans. James Hogarth (New York: Random House Modern Library, 2002), p. 379.

*

HIDDEN BOUNTY -
Epigraph: The quote is falsely attributed to C. G. Jung, despite no documentation for this. Nonetheless, the idea certainly resonates with Jung's theme of the Shadow, which the poem addresses.

*

FAMILIAR FACES –
Epigraph: Debra Dean, *The Madonnas of Leningrad* (New York: Harper Perennial, 2006).

*

UNPERISHING -
Epigraph:
Ursula Vaughan Williams, "The Bird Dream", in *Collected Poems* (London: Albion, 1996), p. 89, v. 15. The experience of mourning as an unfathomable conjunction of the total absence and absolute presence of the deceased—as though death had at last effaced any distance between two souls—is a phenomenon familiar to many who surrender to the gift of grief.

After several decades, I still regret having neglected an invitation to meet with Ursula Vaughan Williams in London, oblivious to the subtle insights and grace of her verses.

*

AUTUMN NOCTURNE -
Epigraph: Novalis, *Hymns to the Night*, 5: "*Die Nacht ward der Offenbarungen mächtiger Schoß.*"

*

EXILE -
Epigraph: ("Harsh is exile") - Salvatore Quasimodo, "Vento a Tíndari", in *The Selected Writings of Salvatore Quasimodo*, trans. Allen Mandelbaum (New York: Noonday-Farrar, Straus, 1960), p. 136, v. 23.
*

FOREVER, EPHEMERAL -
Epigraph: John O'Donohue, *Anam Cara: A Book of Celtic Wisdom* (New York: Harper Perennial, 1998), p. 90.
*

WINTER AFFINITY -
Epigraph: (*...they go not far*) - Salvatore Quasimodo, "I morti",in *The Selected Writings of Salvatore Quasimodo*, trans. Allen Mandelbaum (New York: Noonday-Farrar, Straus, 1960), p. 146, v. 6.
*

A SOLDIER WRITES HOME -
The sonnet weaves and varies the words uttered to me by a veteran as we sat together on a bench during the rain, his words punctuated and illumined by weeping.
*

LACHRIMÆ PAVAN -
Epigraph: John Dowland's "Flow, My Tears", *Second Booke of Songs or Ayres* (London, 1600).
*

*NAFS* -
In the Qur'an and in Sufism, the *nafs* is analogous to the ego, lower self or fallen psyche, which incites the soul to evil. The struggle against the selfish impulses of greed, lust, anger, and perverse fantasies is called *Jihad al-nafs*, or *Jihad al-Akbar*: the great Jihad, the true battle. It is sister to the "Spiritual Combat" in Christian tradition: confronting the demons within, famously treated in the classic spiritual manual *Combattimento spirituale* of Lorenzo Scupoli (c. 1530-1610), published in Venice in 1589, which has since numbered some 600 editions.
*

IN RETROSPECT: DIVORCE -
Epigraph: (*... there will always be mute / beauty and importunate grief.*) "Ma nella notte che varca", *Collected Poems of Lucio Piccolo*, trans. Brian Swann and Ruth Feldman (Princeton, 1972), p. 154.
*

AN ELDER NEARS THE END -
Epigraph: Rumi, *Masnavi* I.15.
*

***FANĀ'*** -
Epigraph: Angelus Silesius, (c. 1624-1677): *Bis daß die Einheit hat verschluckt die Anderheit.* From the couplet "Die volle Seligkeit": Perfect Bliss (or Beatitude, Felicity), in *Cherubinischer Wandersmann*. 1675 (Jena/Leipzig: Eugen Diedrichs, 1905), Bk. 4.10. Though the original is "Until unity has swallowed otherness", I have used Schrady's translation, which inverts the key terms ("*until his otherness is drowned in unity*"); yet her phrase is an

exact mirror of the original, and entirely consonant with the Rheno-Flemish tradition that informs the vision of the Baroque poet-mystic Angelus Silesius (born Johann Scheffler). {cf. *The Cherubinic Wanderer*, trans. Maria Schrady (New York: Paulist P, 1986), 4.10, p. 87.}

My poem embraces the kinship between the Sufi ideal of *fanā'*, the dissolution or annihilation of the ego (*nafs*)—conferring realization of the unity of God, creation, and the individual self—and the Rheno-Flemish tradition exemplified by Meister Eckhart, which often uses the desert as a symbol of the soul plunged into the nothingness of detachment, which Jan van Ruysbroeck calls the "fathomless abyss" of God's love, wherein the soul is "burnt up... undifferentiated and without distinction" (*The Sparkling Stone*, 3).

*

OASIS -

Epigraphs: Plato, *Symposium* 209c; Kathleen Raine, "Night Sky", *Collected Poems* (Washington, D.C.: Counterpoint, 2001), p. 107.

(v. 1-2): The spring stands in contrast to the River Lethe (oblivion), from which the shades in Hades drink to forget their mortal lives. The "waters of remembrance" refer to *anamnesis* (recollection, as opposed to amnesia). In Platonic philosophy, sacred knowledge (*gnosis*) resides in the soul from eternity (*Meno* 86b), and Truth is an unveiling or "unforgetting" (*aletheia*), attained through contemplation (*Phaedo* 66b-d).

(vv. 6-8): The convergence of two gazes epitomizes the communion engendered by the wonder shared in a glimpse of ultimate Beauty: the rigid boundary between self and other melts, the isolated ego is permeated by Spirit, and time penetrated by eternity: in that oasis, both human and nature converge, desert still resonates with its vanished seas. Such visionary knowledge is opposed to the distraction and inattention of ordinary consciousness tainted by fear and fault, provoking a loss of the witnessing and cherishing that consecrate the universal experience of simultaneous Presence and Transcendence.

**V. CANTICUM MYSTERIUM –**

Epigraph: T.S. Eliot, *Four Quartets*, "Little Gidding" (vv. 52-3).

## Publication Acknowledgments

Many thanks go to the editors of the periodicals and volumes in which several poems first appeared:

*Sacred Web* 48 (Winter, 2022): "The Vacant Cross." *Sacred Web* 46 (Winter 2021): "Tabor"; "An Elder Nears the End"; "Perpetual Oblation"; "Matin Bonfire"; "Legible."

*Dappled Things* 13.4 (2018): "Because They Have Forsaken"; "A Garden Regained"; "Angel of the Spandrel"; "Monastery"; *Dappled Things* 10.4 (2015): "Before the Summer."

*Allegro* 11 (UK, 2016). "A Recipe for Sangría"; "A Daughter at the Shore."

*Antiphon* 14 (UK, 2015): "Gull Feather Fallen."

*Grey Sparrow Journal* 6.2 (2015): "Sfumato: Ars Pingendi"; "Crepuscular Flock"; "Aubade"; *Grey Sparrow Journal* 3.3 (2012): "Insatiable."

*Able Muse* 13 (Summer 2012): "An Old Greek Nun Recalls Her Youth."

*Poetry Salzburg Review* 22 (2012): "Winterreise"; "Unholy Territory"; *Poetry Salzburg Review* 16 (2009): "Expectant Autumn."

*Drunken Boat* 16 (2012): "Ananta Raga."

*The Cincinnati Review* 7.2 (2011): "Aperture."

*Oak Bend Review* 5.1 (2009): "Seventy Years."

*Broken Bridge Review* 3 (2008): "Old Ones."

*The Mochila Review* 7 (2005): "Mendocino Vespers" (as "Vespers").

"Exile", in *The Anthology of Monterey Bay Poets*, ed. Ryan Masters (Aptos, CA: Chatoyant P, 2004).

*Romantics Quarterly* 3.1 (2003): "Lux Mundi."

*Full Circle Journal* (Oct. 3, 2003, online): "The Widow Alone."

*Rain City Review* 5 (Portland, OR, 1994/5): "Canticum Mysterium."

"Requiem for a Scholar", in *Saints and their Authors: Studies in Medieval Hispanic Hagiography in Honor of John K. Walsh*, ed. Alan Deyermond, et al. (Madison, WI: Hispanic Seminary of Medieval Studies, 1990).

Zeitfracht Medien GmbH
Ferdinand-Jühlke-Straße 7
99095 Erfurt, Deutschland
produktsicherheit@kolibri360.de